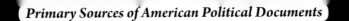
Understanding the
Iroquois
Constitution

James Wolfe and Lesli J. Favor

Enslow Publishing
101 W. 23rd Street
Suite 240
New York, NY 10011
USA

enslow.com

Published in 2016 by Enslow Publishing, LLC.
101 W. 23rd Street, Suite 240, New York, NY 10011

Library of Congress Cataloging-in-Publication Data
Wolfe, James, 1960- author.
 Understanding the Iroquois constitution / James Wolfe and Lesli J. Favor.
   pages cm. — (Primary sources of american political documents)
 Includes bibliographical references and index.
 Summary: "Discusses the creation and execution of the Iroquois Constitution"—Provided by publisher.
 ISBN 978-0-7660-6878-0
 1. Six Nations. Great Law of Peace—Juvenile literature. 2. Iroquois Indians—Legal status, laws, etc.—Juvenile literature 3. Iroquois Indians—Politics and government—Juvenile literature. I. Favor, Lesli J., author. II. Title.
 KIF80.W65 2015
 974.7004'9755—dc23
                              2015008043

Printed in the United States of America

To Our Readers: We have done our best to make sure all Web site addresses in this book were active and appropriate when we went to press. However, the author and the publisher have no control over and assume no liability for the material available on those Web sites or on any Web sites they may link to. Any comments or suggestions can be sent by e-mail to customerservice@enslow.com.

LC: 7/17 Tc: ∅ (3/20)

Contents

Chapter One

The Formation of a Confederacy

*I am Deganawida and with the Five Nations'
Confederate Lords I plant the Tree of Great
Peace. I plant it in your territory, Tadadaho,
and the Onondaga Nation, in the territory of
you who are Fire Keepers . . .*

*Roots have spread out from the Tree of the
Great Peace, one to the north, one to the east,
one to the south, and one to the west. The name
of these roots is The Great White Roots and
their nature is Peace and Strength . . . We place
at the top of the Tree of the Long Leaves an
Eagle who is able to see afar. If he sees in the
distance any evil approaching or any danger
threatening he will at once warn the people of
the Confederacy.*[1]

—From the Iroquois Constitution

Sometime in the late sixteenth century, five Native American tribes living in upstate New York banded together to form a confederacy. The nations that took part were the Mohawk, the Oneida, the Onondaga, the Cayuga, and the Seneca. Together they were known as the Iroquois. The Iroquois Confederacy, or Five Nations Confederacy, was formed in the pursuit of peace, and also to protect the participating tribes against

PRIMARY SOURCE

This map from 1723 shows the land of the Five Nations, or Iroquois. Their territory lies in what is now the state of New York and Canada, in the area around the Great Lakes.

invasion by European interests and other Native American nations.

Conditions Prior to the Confederacy

Before they agreed to form an alliance, terrible warfare existed among the tribes. They clashed over the rights to hunting grounds and fishing areas, and blood feuds grew around acts of revenge and retaliation. The warrior's code of honor required that every attack and killing be avenged. A warrior who did not honor this code was deemed a coward, and those who did honor the code gained prestige and power through their acts. The wars and feuds extended north into the territory of Algonquian-speaking tribes in Canada and east to tribes such as the Mahicans along the Hudson River.

Even at home, safety was not guaranteed. Villages of the same nation dispatched assassins and war parties against one another, and bloody feuds played out for years. Sometimes neighbor fought against neighbor within a village. People stayed inside at night because it was not safe to walk about in darkness. The warfare seemed unstoppable. Violent bloodshed was so commonplace that the Iroquois said, "The sun must love war."

But two Iroquois chiefs, Deganawida (also known as Dekanawidah and Tekanawita) and Hiawatha,

Onondaga chief Hiawatha led the formation of the Iroquois Confederacy, along with Deganawida.

brought a historic change to the five Iroquois nations. Under their leadership, the Iroquois united to form the Five Nations Confederacy. With this, warfare among the Iroquois ended permanently. In 1722 the confederacy adopted a sixth nation, their descendants the Tuscaroras, with whom they shared a common language and culture. The Tuscaroras had lived in territories in the states of North Carolina and Virginia. After the Tuscarora War of 1711 to 1713, they were driven out of the area by English settlers. Most fled north in small groups, eventually gathering in the land of their ancestors, the Iroquois. The Confederacy was thereafter known as the Six Nations Confederacy.

Iroquois Culture

When Deganawida and Hiawatha rose to distinction among the Iroquois, the five nations were living as they had for centuries. The name the Iroquois called themselves—Haudenosaunee, or "People of the Long House"—sets them apart as those who lived in long, bark-covered structures called extended houses, or long houses. A typical long house was about 18 feet (5.5 meters) wide, 18 feet high, and 60 feet (18 meters) long. Some of the largest long houses were around 60 feet (18 meters) wide and over 100 yards (91 meters) long. Holes in the roof let out smoke from cooking fires and let in light. More light poured in through the high doors at each end of the long house. Inside, anywhere from five to twenty related families lived in rooms around the outside walls. They used the space in the center for gatherings and meetings. They constructed their long houses in clusters near sources of water. For protection against attack, they surrounded the village with a sturdy stockade. For added protection,

The Iroquois were known for their long houses. These multi-family dwellings were for sleeping, eating, and meeting.

Long houses had open fires for cooking and holes cut out of the roof to release smoke. Very little light was let in.

some villages dug a moat, a deep trench filled with water, around the outside of the stockade.

The Iroquois culture was matriarchal, meaning that individuals traced their kinship through their mothers. Groups were based on the clan system. Within communities, the primary family unit was an *ohwachira*, a group of relatives usually headed by the clan mother, the oldest living female relative. Two or more ohwachiras formed a clan. Clan members considered each other close family and did not intermarry. When a couple married, the husband joined his wife to live with her ohwachira, and their children took on the clan of their mother. Each clan had the name and symbol of an animal. The Mohawks and Oneidas had three clans: Turtle, Bear, and Wolf. The Onondagas, Cayugas, and Senecas had these three clans as well as others, including Heron, Hawk, Snipe, Beaver, Deer, and Eel.

The clans were headed by chiefs, who worked with chiefs in other clans and villages to govern the tribe as a whole. Women leaders within a clan met together and, with the clan mother, selected their chiefs from among the clan's men. If a chief behaved unwisely and refused the correction of the women leaders and other chiefs, the women had the right to remove him from his position and appoint another person to fill his place. In this way, leadership and power in the tribe was shared by men and women.

Iroquois men and women played equally vital roles in the care and protection of their clans and nations. Men were devoted warriors and hunters. Their primary duties included protecting their village from attack and supplying wild game and fish. Routinely they left their village to make war on another nation or village. Young boys imitated the older men by playing in mock wars and practicing their hunting skills. Women were in charge of the farming, the stores of food, and the long houses. They relied on three main crops: corn, beans, and squash. They called these crops the three sisters. They also cultivated pumpkins and tobacco, and gathered nuts and berries in the forest. During the warm months they dried meat, fish, and vegetables, storing them away for winter. They also filled woven baskets with grain and buried them in the ground until winter.

Deganawida and Hiawatha

Into this setting came Deganawida and Hiawatha. What we know of these leaders comes from accounts and legends passed down by word of mouth over hundreds of years. During the late 1800s and early 1900s, historians began recording some of the legends in writing. The story of the confederacy's founding is called the *Gayaneshakgowa*, or the Great Law of Peace, in Iroquois.

John C. Mohawk, a Seneca scholar of Iroquois history, points out that the Great Law of Peace is so complex that "the tradition that relates it requires over a week in the telling."[2] As might be expected, the various legends differ in places, sometimes greatly. Some contain elements of the supernatural, while others are realistic. But overall, a riveting history-based account emerges, one of good versus evil, peace versus warfare, order versus chaos. The legends center on Deganawida, sometimes called simply the Peacemaker, and Hiawatha.

Deganawida was born to a tribe living north of Lake Ontario in what is present-day Canada. The tribe was a distant relative of the Mohawks: the Wendots, later called Hurons by the French. As the legend goes, before his birth, Deganawida's

This birch bark canoe is typical of the means of transport used by the Hurons, the tribe into which the great leader Deganawida was born.

mother and grandmother had left the Hurons to live in the wilderness because it was too dangerous to live in the villages. A vision came to Deganawida's grandmother telling her that the Creator had made her daughter pregnant with an important child who would grow up to put an end to warfare. Deganawida was born and grew quickly, in supernatural fashion. Soon the women took him to live among the Hurons, where he could spread his message of peace. While playing with other children, Deganawida taught them, "It is sinful for people to hurt one another" and "You should be kind to the people you know as well as to those you don't know."[3] Later, when he was older, he traveled south across Lake Ontario to carry his message of peace to the nations there. For a time he lived among the Mohawks, where he spoke of the Great Law that would come to bring peace to all nations who accepted it.

Hiawatha was a respected chief in the Onondaga Nation, and he too dreamed of peace for his war-torn people. He called all the Onondaga chiefs and people together for a meeting around a great fire, where he would share his ideas. Many Onondagas eagerly attended, for they wondered if this wise leader had found a way to bring peace and safety to their villages. But the council was ill-fated. Chief

HVRONS.

Deganawida's mother believed he would end the warfare that interrupted the Hurons' peaceful existence.

Tadadaho (also known as Adodarhoh) arrived with his devoted warriors. They stalked grimly through the crowd, ready to mark for death anyone who dared cooperate with Hiawatha. Everyone scattered in fear.

Tadadaho was feared throughout all the Iroquois tribes. It was rumored that he was a wizard and that he had supernatural powers. He was said to employ spies and assassins to carry out his wishes. It was

Onondaga chief Tadadaho was feared by his people. He is described as having hair made of snakes and turtle claws for hands.

said that a warrior risked death by speaking above a whisper in his presence. One Iroquois legend, recorded in 1888 by ethnographer J. N. B. Hewitt, describes Tadadaho as a "misshapen monster." He was "a thing—a shape—that was not human but rather supernatural and deformed; for the hair of Tha-do-da-ho was composed of writhing, hissing serpents, his hands were like unto the claws of a turtle, and his feet like unto bear's claws in size."[4] The chief tyrannized and terrorized all the Iroquois.

A Plan for Peace

Tadadaho squelched three attempts by Hiawatha to start peace talks. He did not want his great power as a warrior taken away by peace, and he did not want to bend to the leadership of someone else. After Tadadaho broke up the first council, Hiawatha's oldest daughter died. Then, after Hiawatha called a second council and it, too, was crashed by Tadadaho, Hiawatha's second daughter died. The deaths were blamed on Tadadaho's wizardry. It seemed that peace was doomed to fail.

Hiawatha grieved for his lost daughters, but he refused to give up. For a third time, he called a council. To it he brought his youngest daughter, his only surviving family member, who was expecting a child. While Hiawatha gathered chiefs around the council fire, his daughter helped other women gather firewood nearby. At the fire, Tadadaho suddenly pointed to an eagle flying high above. His warriors shot the eagle and it fell to the ground near Hiawatha's daughter. As the warriors rushed to claim the eagle's prized feathers, Hiawatha's daughter was trampled to death, and her unborn child died with her.

Hiawatha was overcome with grief and rage. In Hewitt's legend he cries, "All my children are now gone from me; they have been destroyed by Tha-do-da-ho, and he has spoiled our plans. It now behooves me to go abroad among other people. I will start now. I will split-the-sky."[5] The phrase "split-the-sky" meant that he would go directly south. And so he left the Onondagas, traveling south across a mountain, a lake, and another mountain. Then he turned east.

Hiawatha feared that he was losing his mind in his rage at losing everyone he had loved. He gathered rushes, plants with round stems that grow in wet areas, and used them to make three strings of beads. He hung the strings of beads before him and, staring at the beads, thought of his grief. He decided that if he met another person with grief such as his, he would use strings like these to represent words of comfort to him. In this way, some say, the Iroquois tradition of the Condolence Council began. In this ceremony, special representatives comfort mourners using songs and strings of beads.

Hiawatha wandered eastward, across Onondaga territory and then across that of the Oneida. In time he came to Mohawk territory, where small lakes dotted the landscape. On their shores, he gathered small white shells and strung them together to form strings, which he draped around his neck as a sign of peace.

By this time, Deganawida was living among the Mohawk. When Hiawatha came to his village, he took the grief-torn wanderer in. With great interest he listened to Hiawatha tell how he had tried to introduce peace to his tribe but had failed because of Tadadaho. In Hiawatha, Deganawida recognized a kindred spirit. They both sought to end warfare. They decided that together they would unite the Iroquois nations in a confederacy of peace. In a legend dictated by Seneca chief John A. Gibson in 1912, Deganawida says, "It will stop, the way in which matters are proceeding here on earth beneath the sky, such that they cause pools and streams of human blood to flow . . . it will stop, human beings killing one another and also scalping one another . . ."[6]

At the heart of Deganawida's plan for peace was an idea that all the nations would join together as one family. From then on, they would be brothers and sisters to one another regardless of nation. Just as they had loyalty to their own clan, they would now have loyalty to all members of the confederacy. Each clan in one tribe would unite as family with the clan of the same name in the other tribes. For example, the Wolf clan in the Mohawk Nation would become family with the Wolf clans in the other nations. The bonds of family would be honored to such an extent that members of the Wolf clan would not inter-marry, even between tribes. Deganawida won the Mohawks' approval of his plan for the confederacy. Now he had to convince the chiefs of the other nations to unite with them.

Deganawida journeyed west with Hiawatha to Oneida territory. They expected this nation to be receptive to the plan for a confederacy, for they had suffered terribly from Onondaga warriors. The leading Oneida chief, Odatshedeh, listened carefully to Deganawida and Hiawatha. He told them that he must consider the idea for a day. According to traditional Iroquois political speech,

After meeting up with Deganawida, Hiawatha traveled to other nations, proposing a peaceful confederacy.

by saying "a day" the chief meant a year. Although it must have been difficult to be patient, Deganawida and Hiawatha waited a year, and then they returned to Odatshedeh. It was a momentous occasion, for he had decided to join the confederacy. The legend published by Horatio Hale in 1882 proclaimed, "The treaty which initiated the great league was then and there ratified between the representatives of the Mohawk and Oneida Nations."[7]

Next, Deganawida and Hiawatha went to the Onondaga. Here they faced the unrelenting power of Tadadaho, who had stopped Hiawatha's peace talks three times. Tadadaho listened to Deganawida and Hiawatha with a cold and surly demeanor. He flatly rejected the idea of joining the confederacy, and the other chiefs feared to cross him. The peacemakers left, moving westward, but they harbored hope that they would find a way to win over Tadadaho.

It yet remained to present the message of peace to the Cayuga and the Seneca. The Cayuga received Deganawida and Hiawatha's message with good will. After long years of suffering attacks by the Onondaga, they welcomed the idea of a peaceful and protective confederacy. With this news gladdening their hearts, Deganawida and Hiawatha moved on to the Seneca. Unfortunately, Seneca

This Onondaga descendant would have grown up learning the story of Tadadaho and Hiawatha.

chiefs were divided in their response. Some wanted to join the confederacy, but the head warrior and his deputy did not. The nation could not reach a consensus. Hopeful that the factions could resolve their disagreement, Deganawida and Hiawatha urged them to work out their differences.

A Second Chance at Tadadaho

After that, Deganawida and Hiawatha turned their attention back to the Onondaga. As long as Tadadaho opposed them, the confederacy would have a gaping hole in its middle, for Onondaga territory formed the geographical center of the five tribes. It was vital to win Tadadaho's cooperation. The peacemakers devised a savvy plan by which to gain their opponent's wholehearted support.

They returned to Tadadaho. Some legends record how Daganawida and Hiawatha tamed the beastly chief with spiritual ceremonies, setting his mind and body straight again from its twisted, evil nature. Deganawida sang songs to Tadadaho to regenerate his crazed mind and bring it back to a state of reason and humanity. He performed a healing ceremony on the misshapen body of Tadadaho so his feet, hands, and hair were once again natural and human. Everyone marveled at the changes in the once-terrible chief. In Hewitt's legend they exclaim, "We have now redeemed Tha-da-da-ho."[8]

Now that Tadadaho had been redeemed mentally and physically, Deganawida spoke again of the confederacy. He used political reasoning to persuade the powerful chief to join. Fifty chiefs, called sachems, would form the Grand Council of the confederacy, and Tadadaho would be made the head sachem. He alone would have the power to call councils, and the main Onondaga village would be the meeting place. The Onondaga Nation would be represented in the council by fourteen sachems, while no other tribe would have more than ten. Finally, Tadadaho would have the right to veto any act or decision of the council. They had taken a risk by proposing the terms of the council in this way, but they knew what they were doing. Under the terms of the confederacy, all the tribes would be one family. Once Tadadaho took leadership of this extended family, he would protect and direct it with the same care he would give his own clan. And in the end, the Peacemaker was successful. Tadadaho agreed to the plan, and the Onondaga joined the confederacy.

The league was complete when, at last, the Seneca joined. To persuade the Seneca to set aside

Grassit St Sauveur inv direx   J. Laroque Sculp.

With the joining of the Onondaga, Seneca, Mohawk, Oneida, and Cayuga, the Five Nations, or Iroquois confederacy, was born. The Iroquois became a strong and powerful people. They were known for taking in those who were displaced and offering shelter to those who were lost.

their differences, the two leading Seneca chiefs had been given the positions of head war chiefs of the league.

Finally the chiefs of the five nations convened beneath a great pine tree, which became the symbol of the Five Nations Confederacy. Deganawida named it the Tree of the Great Long Leaves and called its roots the Great White Roots. These roots were said to grow in four directions—north, south, east, and west—representing the law of the confederacy extending in all directions. At the top of this pine tree perched an eagle, whose piercing gaze monitored the land. If danger or evil threatened, the eagle would warn the confederacy. Beneath the Tree of the Great Long Leaves, the chiefs united to join their nations as one family in one symbolic long house—the confederacy. Deganawida charged the chiefs with steadfast loyalty to one another, urging them to join their arms so firmly that, should a tree fall upon their clasped arms, it would not separate them. In this unwavering solidarity the confederacy would thrive and prosper in coming years.

A great alliance was born. The five nations would one day welcome a sixth. They would band together to play an important role in the future of North America.

Chapter Two

The Establishment of the Great Law of Peace

All the business of the Five Nations Confederate Council shall be conducted by the two combined bodies of Confederate Lords. First the question shall be passed upon by the Mohawk and Seneca Lords, then it shall be discussed and passed by the Oneida and Cayuga Lords. Their decisions shall then be referred to the Onondaga Lords, (Fire Keepers) for final judgment.

When a case comes before the Onondaga Lords (Fire Keepers) for discussion and decision, Tadadaho shall introduce the matter to his comrade Lords who shall then discuss it in their two bodies. Every Onondaga Lord except Hononwiretonh shall deliberate and he shall listen only. When a unanimous decision shall have been reached by the two bodies of Fire Keepers, Tadadaho shall notify Hononwiretonh of the fact when he shall confirm it. He shall refuse to confirm a decision if it is not unanimously agreed upon by both sides of the Fire Keepers.[1]

—From the Iroquois Constitution

The union that resulted from the Great Peace was the first of its kind in North America. But exactly when this monumental union occurred is a matter of debate. In J.N.B. Hewitt's "Legend of the

Created in the 1980s, the flag of the Iroquois Nation is based on Hiawatha's wampum belt. The white pine tree of peace, whose needles grow in clusters of five, is remembered as the place under which members of the five nations buried their weapons.

Founding of the Iroquois League," the ethnographer refers to the date as simply "in the times of our forefathers."[2] Many scholars use a 1535 recorded entry by Jacques Cartier, the French explorer, as a reference point, as it is believed the confederacy was established before this time. Other historians believe the union occurred much earlier, closer to 1400.

Deganawida presided over the first meeting of the sachems of the Five Nations Confederacy, and he is credited with creation of the ideas found in the Great Law of Peace. The Great Law was unique in American history in that it was the first organized law to set up a confederacy governed by democratic principles. It brought together independent nations into one political body governed by an organized group of representatives. The Great Law touched on all areas of Iroquois life, beginning with the uniting of the five warring nations in a new peace. But it was more than just a peace treaty. It was a long and complex law that set up the manner in which sachems would be appointed and how they would lead the nations. Provisions for treason and succession were outlined, as well as the rights of members and nonmembers, clan matters, defense,

Jacques Cartier (1491–1557) encountered the Iroquois on his many voyages to America.

and emigration. On a more personal level, matters of birth, religion, adoption, and death were addressed.

The Grand Council

For their first council, the confederate sachems convened beneath the Tree of the Great Long Leaves. Standing before them, Deganawida spoke. He narrated the Great Law of Peace, or Gayaneshakgowa, which codified the confederation's system of government, fundamental laws, and guiding principles. The Great Law is sometimes called the Iroquois Constitution. It was the first American political document to provide advisory councils, leaders responsible to the larger community, and integral roles for women in the government of the union.

During negotiations to bring the Onondaga into the confederation, Tadadaho had been named head sachem of the council. Deganawida confirmed this appointment in the Great Law. In addition, the Onondagas were named the Fire Keepers of the council, for all councils would convene in their territory. Onondaga land was designated the capital of the confederacy, and the wampum belts and other symbols of the council and its traditions were to be kept by the Onondaga. In short, the Onondaga territory was the seat of Iroquois government, just as Washington DC is the seat of the United States government.

One of Deganawida's first orders of business was to create the Grand Council of the confederacy. On this council would sit fifty sachems, sometimes called lords or simply chiefs. The sachems would represent their respective nations in political decisions and actions of the confederacy. At the first council, the fifty confederate lords were chosen and appointed to their positions. One by one, each of the chosen men stood with his clan mother

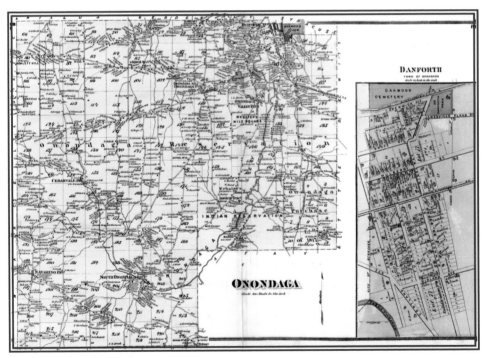

This 1874 map shows Onondaga County in New York. This territory was selected as the capital of the Iroquois confederacy.

before Deganawida. Deganawida and the clan mother crowned the sachem with the antlers of a deer, the symbol of his position. Their titles would be hereditary, held by the head women of the clans. Upon a sachem's death or removal from office, the clan mother, with the advice and approval of clan leaders, would select his successor from the same clan.

With the appointment of the fifty sachems, the Great Council was complete. The council would serve as the principal lawmaking body of the Five Nations Confederacy. The number of council seats allotted to each nation was decided by Deganawida and was permanent. Most highly represented was the Onondaga tribe, with fourteen sachems. Next was the Cayuga with ten sachems, the Mohawk with nine, the Oneida with nine, and the Seneca with eight.

Other Appointments

In addition to the fifty sachems, Deganawida appointed five war chiefs, one per nation, to lead the confederacy in times of war and to serve as liaisons between the Grand Council and the people of each nation. War chiefs were chosen from the young men of the families of the confederate lords, and the title of war chief, like that of confederate lord, was hereditary. Specifically, the women who were heirs of the confederate lords' titles were also heirs of the war chiefs' titles and would nominate successors to the positions when necessary. The war chiefs' duties were to organize and command the confederacy's warriors, to carry messages between the council lords and their respective nations, and to observe council meetings. If a war chief or any person from his nation suspected an error in council proceedings, then the war chief was to speak with one of the lords of his nation about it. He was also the intermediary by which people could communicate their questions, concerns, and suggestions to the council. The women leaders of the clan conveyed warnings to the lords of their nation through their war chief. Like a sachem, a war chief who violated the codes of conduct for his office forfeited his title, which would be stripped from him and given to another person.

In addition to establishing hereditary titles in the Iroquois government, Deganawida made provisions for pine tree chiefs. These chiefs were selected on the basis of wisdom, honesty, trustworthiness, and devotion to the good of the Confederacy. Once appointed, a pine tree chief could not be removed from the position—"no one shall cut him down,"[3] says the Constitution. But in effect, an errant chief would be powerless, for his advice, opinions, and suggestions would be ignored. Unlike the position of council sachem, the pine tree chief's position was not hereditary.

The Five Nations Governing Structure

Deganawida set up a political structure whereby the five nations would be governed. He divided the league into moieties, or subdivisions. In one moiety were the Onondaga, Mohawk, and Seneca, called the Older Brothers. In the other moiety were the Oneida and Cayuga, called the Younger Brothers. The seating arrangement at council meetings was arranged according to these divisions. The fourteen Onondaga sachems, as Fire Keepers, sat at the head of the council fire. To their right sat the Mohawk and Seneca sachems. To the left of the Fire Keepers sat the Oneida and Cayuga sachems.

To make decisions and settle political questions, the council functioned in three-part structure. The Onondaga held the ultimate power of approval or veto. The Mohawk and Seneca formed the second group, with the Oneida and Cayuga forming the third. Although the Onondaga Lords were the Fire Keepers and had the power of veto and final decision regarding split opinions, the Constitution named the Mohawk as "the heads and leaders"[4] of the confederacy. The presence of all Mohawk lords was required for council meetings to be legal. Moreover, if the Mohawk lords opposed any resolution, it could not be passed. The Constitution explained the Mohawks' right to these powers by stating, "The Mohawk Lords are the foundation of the Great Peace,"[5] referring to Deganawida and Hiawatha, who had been adopted into the Mohawk Nation.

Council Meetings

Next, Deganawida specified the tradition by which the Onondaga leader would open each Grand Council meeting. First he would greet the lords of the Five Nations and express gratitude at their presence. Then he would deliver a ceremonious speech that centered the attention of those in attendance on the principles forming the heart of Iroquois society, including gratitude and respect for the earth and its resources of animals, crops, fruits, plants, and water. The speaker would also offer thanks to the Great Creator, "who dwells in the heavens above, who gives all the things useful to men, and who is the source and the ruler of health and life."[6] After this address, matters of business began, which were handled according to a standard procedure.

All matters brought before the council were taken up by the Mohawk lords first. These nine lords were divided into three groups of three. The third group listened as the first two groups discussed the matter at hand. They spoke only to identify a suspected error in the work of the first two groups. When the first two groups reached a decision, the third group confirmed it and passed it to the Seneca lords for their review.

The Seneca lords then considered the matter, working toward a consensus with the Mohawk. When the Mohawk and Seneca reached a consensus, they passed their opinion to the Younger Brothers. If the Oneida and Cayuga agreed with the opinion, they passed the matter back to the Mohawk, who formally announced the decision to the Onondaga. Finally, the Onondaga reviewed the opinion. If they agreed with it, they confirmed and approved the matter.

This system of checks and balances meant that, ideally, matters ratified by the council were unanimously approved by all five nations. If there was disagreement, the lords discussed it until they reached consensus. However, the Constitution made provisions for situations in which a consensus could not be reached. For example, if the Mohawks presented an opinion to the Seneca, but the two groups could not agree, they passed both opinions to the Younger Brothers. First the Oneida evaluated the opinion. If they, too, were divided on the matter, they passed both opinions to the Cayuga. If the opinion was still split, they returned it to the Mohawk, who announced the split opinion to the Onondaga. The Onondaga had the authority to break the tie, choosing one opinion or the other. Some accounts of the Great Law indicate that if the Onondaga believed harm could come from either opinion, they could choose not to approve either but instead return the matter to the other tribes to be reworked.

Deganawida's Great Law also outlines the procedures to be followed during the serious illness or death of a council sachem. When a sachem became deathly ill and clearly would not recover, the antlers symbolizing his position on the Grand Council were ritually removed and set aside. To represent the removing of the antlers, a title wampum, or string of shell beads symbolizing the title, was given to a representative of his moiety. The antlers, or lordship, were not to pass into death with him. At this time also a strand of dark wampum was hung near his head. If the sachem unexpectedly recovered, then the title was bestowed again upon him. But if he died, the dark wampum was taken down and used as the "invitation wampum" to activate the Condolence Council.

The Condolence Council was a special ceremony held to comfort the lords of the moiety who suffered the loss and to appoint a successor to the title. For example, if a Mohawk lord died, the Condolence Council was formed of the Oneida and Cayuga lords, and the women who held the Mohawk lord's title nominated a successor. The consolation ceremony was a "reading" of the thirteen wampum strings of Hiawatha. The rite of Conferring the Lordship Title was held to induct the new lord into office.

Wampum Belts

Until Europeans began creating dictionaries of Iroquois languages in the early 1800s, the Iroquois had no written language. They relied heavily on oral tradition to preserve the Great Law, their histories, and their legends for succeeding generations. They used specially made wampum belts whose patterns of beads formed a record of Iroquois governmental tradition. During council meetings, chiefs could refer to the belts for reminders of legal procedures and other key elements of Iroquois law. The Iroquois Constitution itself is rich in imagery and symbolism to help communicate the dignity, respect, and value of the confederacy, its lords, and its laws and traditions.

Special symbols were placed next to Tadadaho when he sat at the head of the council fire. Beside him was placed a white mat, and on the mat was laid a bird's wing. Beside them were two poles standing upright in the ground with a crosspiece spanning their tops. On the crosspiece hung wampum that represented Tadadaho's power. Other legends and versions of the Constitution further describe the meanings of these pieces. The white mat is sometimes said to be a wide, white wampum belt that represents peace and purity. The feather, or Long Wing, is for sweeping away impurities from the belt. A pole or staff symbolizes a tool with which to chase away harm or threats to the league.

Another symbol represented the solidarity and loyalty of the nations of the league: a bundle of five arrows, one arrow from each of the five nations. Together, the arrows represented the unified strength of the confederacy. Each arrow alone may be easily broken, but when bound together the arrows are too strong to break. The bundle of arrows reminded the Iroquois nations that separately they were vulnerable, but together they were strong. Many years later, when the United States was forming, its leaders chose symbols like those of the Iroquois Confederacy—an eagle and a bundle of arrows. In the US version, an eagle clutches a bundle of thirteen arrows, one for each of the thirteen colonies.

Deganawida proclaimed at the first council that any lord could make wampum belts as records of important national or international matters. Wampum belts and strings were especially important symbols of league ceremonies, traditions, and values. Some of the belts made by lords of the confederacy have been preserved and passed down through the generations as Iroquois national treasures. The special wampum belts created to record the Great Law and its traditions are similar in value and meaning to American symbols such as the flag, the Liberty Bell, and the United States Constitution.

One of these treasured wampum belts is the Circlet of the League Wampum, shaped in a circle with fifty strands pointing inward. The perimeter of the circle was formed of two strings of wampum

These wampum belts tell the history and philosophy of the Iroquois. They are woven with wampum, shell beads found on the North Atlantic coast that were also used as currency.

twisted together, one to represent the Great Peace and the other to represent the Great Law. The circular shape symbolizes the circle of protection formed by the confederate lords around the member nations. The fifty wampum strings represent the fifty lords who stand together, arms linked, to protect and guide the people. A chief who disregards the laws of the council is said to move outside the circle; his antlers, symbolizing his title, are caught and held by the circle of lords so that the hereditary title remains in the confederacy. The lord who steps outside the circle forfeits his right to position and power. By the time of the American Revolution, the Circlet of the League Wampum was already a treasured symbol to the Confederacy, and it was moved during this time to Canada.

Another special wampum belt, the Hiawatha Belt, celebrates the formation of the league. In the center of the belt is a pine tree representing the Onondaga Nation, where the confederacy met beneath the Tree of the Great Long Leaves. On each side of the pine tree are two squares formed of white wampum beads, joined together with a double row of white beads; the inner squares join to the pine tree with a single row of white beads. The four squares are said to represent the Mohawk,

Oneida, Cayuga, and Seneca Nations. It is estimated that this wampum belt was made in the 1600s. The belt was kept and displayed, along with other Iroquois belts, by the New York State Museum in Albany. On October 21, 1989, a dozen wampum belts, including the Hiawatha Belt, were returned to the Onondaga.

With the establishment of the Great Peace, an important question remained. What would the chiefs do with their weapons and traditions of warfare? They and their forefathers had fought fiercely with heavy war clubs that could split a skull with a single blow, and with sharp weapons that could cut the scalp from a victim or slash his throat. The chiefs agreed that there was no place for such weapons of destruction in the new league of peace. Deganawida proposed a fitting solution. They would bury their weapons beneath the Tree of the Great Long Leaves, the tree of peace. The legends describe how they dug deep beneath the tree and threw their weapons into the pit, where the waters of the earth carried them away. Then they covered the hole over. Now the five nations would share hunting grounds and fishing areas. Men could hunt and women could tend crops without fear of attack.

Despite its name, the Great Law of Peace was not intended to end warfare altogether. While it bound the five participating nations to maintain peace with one another, it did not prohibit them from fighting other nations. In fact, the pact created a strong unified force against such attacks and from any other threatening outsider.

The Iroquois confederacy created a stronger, unified force against other attacking nations, as with this French attack on an Onondaga village in 1615.

Chapter Three

The Power of the Iroquois Constitution

Whenever a specially important matter or a great emergency is presented before the Confederate Council and the nature of the matter affects the entire body of the Five Nations . . . then the Lords of the Confederacy must submit the matter to the decision of their people and the decision of the people shall affect the decision of the Confederate Council. This decision shall be a confirmation of the voice of the people.

All the Clan council fires of a nation or of the Five Nations may unite into one general council fire, or delegates from all the council fires may be appointed to unite in a general council for discussing the interests of the people. The people shall have the right to make appointments and to delegate their power to others of their number.[1]

—From the Iroquois Constitution

When US history books tell the story of the framing of the US Constitution, they focus on the Founding Fathers' insistence on a government through representation. The framers of the constitution were greatly influenced by European philosophers who emphasized individual rights. But the US Constitution may also owe some of its content and principles to the Iroquois Constitution.

The Iroquois Constitution established a representative government for the five Iroquois nations. Not only is each nation represented by a guaranteed number of sachems on the Confederacy Council, but provisions are made for war chiefs and pine tree chiefs to have voices in government as well. On the level of the common people, further provisions for representation are built into the Constitution. Men and women in every clan can gather to discuss the interests and welfare of the people of their clan.

The Constitution orders separate council fires for the women and the men in each clan. Here they can gather to confer about the clan's interests, welfare, and needs. If they want to convey decisions or suggestions to the Confederacy Council, the war chief of their nation carries the message. The clans also have the right to assemble with other clans in

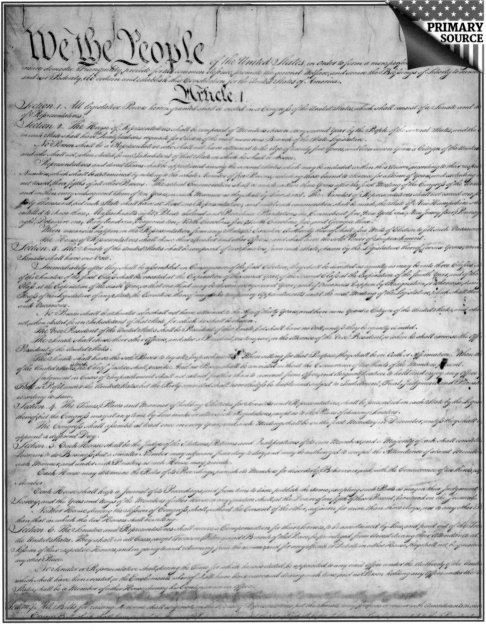

It is believed that the Founding Fathers may have used many ideas taken from the Iroquois Constitution when they were drafting the Constitution of the United States in 1787.

their nation or with the clans in all five nations to discuss the welfare of the people. War chiefs carry decisions and suggestions from these councils to the Confederacy Council. In these ways, the proposals of people at the lowest level are brought to the lords at the highest level of government.

The Iroquois Government and the US Government

The Iroquois Constitution preserves the traditional governmental system of the individual nations. In the past, each nation had its own council fire at which the nation's leaders met and made decisions for the nation. The Iroquois Constitution guarantees continuation of these councils in the new confederacy. The chiefs of each nation continue to govern their own nations, but they govern according to the laws, principles, and intent of the Iroquois Constitution. The individual Iroquois nations are like US states. Each has rights and responsibilities, but reports to and cooperates with the higher, confederate level of government.

The Grand Council has a tripartite structure comprised of the Fire Keepers, the Older Brothers, and the Younger Brothers. This structure distributes power and authority in a system of checks and balances. In some ways the US government, as outlined in the Constitution of 1787, bears similarities to the Iroquois Grand Council. The legislative branch (Congress) is divided into the upper house (Senate) and the lower house (House of Representatives). On the Grand Council, the Older Brothers (Mohawk and Seneca) are like an upper house, or the Senate. The Younger Brothers (Oneida and Cayuga) are like a lower house, or the House of Representatives. Both groups on the council report to and confer with the Fire Keepers, the Onondaga. The Fire Keepers are like the executive branch of our government, headed by the president.

Just as the Senate and the House debate bills and motions, so did the Older and Younger Brothers. Just as Congress passes its recommendations and decisions to the executive branch of government, so did the Older and Younger Brothers pass their opinions to the Onondaga. The Onondaga have the authority to cast a tie-breaking vote in the case of a split decision coming from the Older and Younger Brothers. But the Iroquois did not place one sachem at the head of the entire government, as the American president is placed. The Onondaga as a group are heads of the council, but the Mohawk

Like that of the Iroquois, the US government distributed power with a system of checks and balances.

sachems have the power of veto, for a law cannot be passed if they object to it.

The Status of Women Under the Iroquois Constitution

One of the most distinctive aspects of the Iroquois Constitution was its provisions for the social and political powers of women. To a degree, the Constitution reflects the social status that Iroquois women always held. Kinship is traced through the mother's family, and families related through their women share a long house. It was logical in this society, in which women already held status as clan leaders, to give women the rights to nominate chiefs, hold political councils, and reprimand or remove errant chiefs. Moreover, the Constitution specifies that women are the landowners. "In them is it vested as a birthright . . . They shall own the land and the soil."[2]

Under the Constitution, strings of wampum were given to the women of the families holding a hereditary title to the Grand Council. These women were declared Royaneh, or noble. The wampum strings represent the title and are passed down through the female line. Legally, only the women who hold the strings may bestow the title upon a man. According to the Constitution, "The strings shall be the token that the females of the family have the proprietary right to the Lordship title for all time to come."[3] It is the women who hold the title, and they vest their power in the leaders whom they choose.

Just as the women could bestow the lordship title, so they could take away the title in the case of certain offenses. One serious offense was neglecting the duty of attending Grand Council meetings. The Constitution specified that if a Lord "neglects or refuses to attend the Confederate Council,"[4] then the other lords of his nation should speak to their war chief. The war chief, in turn, will speak with the women leaders of the offending lord's clan. The women leaders will officially reprimand the lord and order him to attend the council. The women's warning and order to attend the council was not to be taken lightly and would be issued only once. If after this the lord did not attend, the women would strip him of his title and assign it to another man of the same clan.

Other serious offenses were breaking the laws of the Constitution and neglecting the welfare of the people. In the case of these offenses, the men or women of the lord's clan had the right to complain to the lord's war chief, who would reprimand the errant lord. If the lord ignored the reprimand, it was issued again. If that was ignored, a third and final reprimand was required. If the lord still ignored the warning of his people and war chief, the women of the clan could take action. They would authorize the war chief to remove the lord's title, and the lords of the council sanctioned the act. The lord's antlers, the emblem of his lordship, were ceremoniously removed and returned to the women heirs of the title.

The offense of murder was so serious that a lord guilty of murder was not only stripped of his title but was cast out of the confederacy and its territories. The women relatives of the murderer were stripped of their possession of the title. Female leaders of a "sister family," or closely related family, were given possession of and responsibility for the title. A sister family might also receive the title if the female relatives of the family holding the title died out.

The Iroquois Constitution and the Albany Congress

With its civic principles, government, and laws, the Iroquois Confederacy planted deep roots of democracy in North America well before English colonists arrived and began dreaming of their own democratic union. When Europeans did arrive and begin interacting with the Iroquois and other American Indian groups, the Iroquois willingly shared their ideas for political union and democracy with colonial leaders. For example, colonial leaders invited Iroquois Confederate lords to attend historic meetings such as the Albany Congress of 1754, at which the Albany Plan of Union was debated, and meetings and debates surrounding the writing of the Articles of Confederation and the Declaration of Independence.

Scholars have studied the ways in which ideas in the Iroquois Constitution may have influenced the founders of the United States and their ideas for shaping the new democracy. As early as 1754, Benjamin Franklin studied the strengths of the Iroquois Confederacy and referred to it when he proposed his Albany Plan of Union. He said, "It would be a strange thing if six nations of ignorant savages should be capable of forming a scheme for such a union and be able to execute it in such a manner as that it has subsisted ages and appears insoluble; and yet that a like union should be impracticable for ten or a dozen English colonies."[5]

In the summer of 1754, the Iroquois Confederacy sent approximately 150 representatives to a

Ben Franklin's famous ultimatum, "Join or Die," which urged the thirteen colonies to unite against England's tyranny, was inspired by the Iroquois Confederacy.

meeting of colonial leaders in Albany, New York. One of these Iroquois leaders was Theyanoguin, a Mohawk who had been a lord on the Grand Council since about 1710. For decades Theyanoguin had been one of the foremost leaders of the Iroquois, much respected among them for his diplomatic and leadership abilities. The English called him Hendrick or King Hendrick. Theyanoguin and the other Iroquois leaders listened carefully to what Benjamin Franklin and other colonial leaders had to say at the Albany Congress.

One purpose of the Albany Congress was to unite the British colonies in a common defense against the French, who were in competition with Great Britain for control of territory in North America. At the congress, the colonies sought the alliance of the Iroquois Confederacy against the French. But Theyanoguin and the other Iroquois leaders did not commit to such an alliance.

Nevertheless, certain aspects of the Iroquois union of nations influenced the Albany Congress's efforts to devise a union for the American colonies. Benjamin Franklin, who drafted the Albany Plan of Union, drew inspiration from the Iroquois league. The colonies would retain their individual constitutions, as did the Iroquois nations, and

Iroquois leader Theyanoguin, or King Hendrick to the English, used his considerable diplomatic talents to maintain an alliance with the British in order to preserve Mohawk interests.

they would select representatives to sit on a grand council. Franklin proposed a union to be headed by a president-general who would report to the British Crown. Each of the colonies would elect men to the union's grand council, their numbers based upon population. But Franklin believed that a wholesale replication of the Iroquois Constitution would not serve the needs of the colonies. Whereas the Iroquois Constitution vests its power and authority in fifty sachems, Franklin believed that the colonies would be better served by having executive power vested in a single person, the president-general.

Influence on the US Constitution

Although the Albany Congress adopted Franklin's plan, the British government and its colonial governors did not. Nothing more came of the plan, although it stands as one of the documents that inspired the United States Constitution. Franklin was an active member of the Constitutional Convention in 1787, helping to write the US Constitution. Undeniably, the content of the US Constitution was determined in part by European and classical influences. But, in its system of representation, checks and balances, and democratic principles, the democracy codified by

English philosopher John Locke (1632–1704) is credited with inspiring many of the ideas used in writing both the Declaration of Independence and the Constitution of the United States. Locke believed in a separation of powers within a government and believed in the rights of the individual.

the United States Constitution also bears some resemblance to the Great Law of the Iroquois.

Scholars disagree over the extent of influence of the Iroquois Constitution on the US Constitution. Those who believe that there was a direct influence point to colonial leaders such as Franklin, John Adams, Thomas Jefferson, George Washington, and others who met with Iroquois leaders, discussed political ideas with them, and observed or read about their government. Many scholars believe that the Iroquois are to be counted among the political thinkers who, along with European thinkers such as John Locke and Jean-Jacques Rousseau, contributed to the formation of American democracy.

On the other hand, some scholars are not convinced that the contact between Iroquois and colonial leaders was far-reaching enough to have influenced the formation of the US Constitution. They acknowledge the contact between Iroquois and colonial leaders, but they assert it was not extensive enough to have amounted to a real influence of one society's government on that of the other. Moreover, they point out that the Iroquois Constitution was not put into writing until the late 1800s, long after the US Constitution had been written in 1787. They suggest that during the

The philosophies of Jean-Jacques Rousseau (1712–1778) also were on the framer's minds when they drafted the constitution. Rousseau's ideas influenced the French Revolution, as well.

intervening century, elements of the US document may have seeped into the oral tradition of the Iroquois document. The influence, in that case, would flow in the opposite direction.

Regardless of its degree of influence on the US Constitution, the Iroquois Constitution is a powerful pact whose democratic ideals are echoed in many of the documents that the founding fathers created when establishing the United States of America. The Iroquois Confederacy was formed and its constitution in use by the time European settlements were established on the Eastern seaboard. Though the Europeans may have considered the Iroquois ignorant and barbaric, they certainly admired their government structure and laws when it came time to establish an independent democratic nation.

Chapter Four

The Legacy of the Iroquois Confederacy

Every five years the Five Nations Confederate Lords and the people shall assemble together and shall ask one another if their minds are still in the same spirit of unity for the Great Binding Law and if any of the Five Nations shall not pledge continuance and steadfastness to the pledge of unity then the Great Binding Law shall dissolve.

Five arrows shall be bound together very strong and each arrow shall represent one nation. As the five arrows are strongly bound this shall symbolize the complete union of the nations. Thus are the Five Nations united completely and enfolded together, united into one head, one body and one mind. Therefore they shall labor, legislate and council together for the interest of future generations.[1]

—*From the Iroquois Constitution*

The Iroquois Constitution has been challenged several times throughout its history. The arrival of Europeans was responsible for many of those challenges. Once European explorers began settling and trading in their territory, around the mid 1530s, the Iroquois began to depend on their goods. This manifested itself in Iroquois raids on other tribes who exchanged goods with the Europeans. They kidnapped and killed members of these tribes, returning with stolen axes, metal armor, and tools. When they embarked on direct trade with French, Dutch, and English explorers and settlers over the next two centuries, they also negotiated treaties. This resulted in a long-running peace with the Dutch and English, and also in great leverage and power for the Iroquois Confederacy. However, once North America began to be organized into colonies and then into an independent nation, that power was threatened.

In the early years, however, the Iroquois were a great force to be reckoned with in the regions south and east of the Great Lakes. The five, and later six, tribes were united loyally under the Iroquois Constitution. Although their desire was to spread the Great Peace, they offered it with strings attached. Peace would be established only on their terms and under their constitution. In this respect outside tribes easily could have viewed acceptance of the Great Peace as defeat. After all, the Iroquois Constitution demands submission to the Iroquois' political and social systems, and nonconformity results in expulsion of the nation from the confederacy.

Compounding the problem is the fact that a new tribe admitted to the confederacy has no right to seats on the Grand Council. These seats are fixed at fifty, and they belong to the head women of the five founding tribes. As the Constitution puts it, "Aliens have nothing by blood to make claim to a vote."[2] The Tuscarora, the only tribe to be adopted into the confederacy after the original five, hold no seats on the council.

Moreover, the Iroquois were not content simply to invite other tribes to join the confederacy. They were willing—and indeed devoted—to spreading the Great Peace by force. The constitution sanctions war against tribes who do not willingly accept the Great Law to "establish the Great Peace by a conquest of the rebellious nation."[3]

Tied up in their interest in spreading the Great Law to other nations was the desire of the Iroquois to protect their own borders. Despite their great unity against outsiders, the tribes were subject to periodic enemy raids. Retaliation for these attacks was an opportunity for warriors to gain and strengthen their status, since prestige and power were earned mostly in warfare. While Iroquois men earned some respect through hunting and fishing, these seasonal activities could not provide the same opportunities for glory as battle could. With peace among the Iroquois nations, the warriors looked outside their borders for distinction and fame. Not only did they defend their borders, they sought to expand their territory by conquering other tribes.

European Settlers

The arrival of Europeans brought additional conflict. At first, the Europeans only explored the land and traded with natives. Arriving in Canada in 1534, French explorer Jacques Cartier led a group along the St. Lawrence River. Other exploratory journeys followed. When the French began trading with natives living along the river, trade goods made their way into the tribes of the region. Iroquois war parties raided those tribes, seizing trade goods and wreaking havoc in French trade relations with those peoples. The French quickly grew weary of Iroquois disruption of trade and began to ally themselves with the Algonquian-speaking peoples of the region. Together they formed a new force against the Iroquois.

In the early 1600s, the Dutch began exploring and trading with natives along the Hudson River, including the Mahicans, whose territory lay to the east of the Mohawk Nation. They offered axes, hoes, kettles and knives, in exchange for beaver skins. As in the north, Iroquois warriors began raiding the

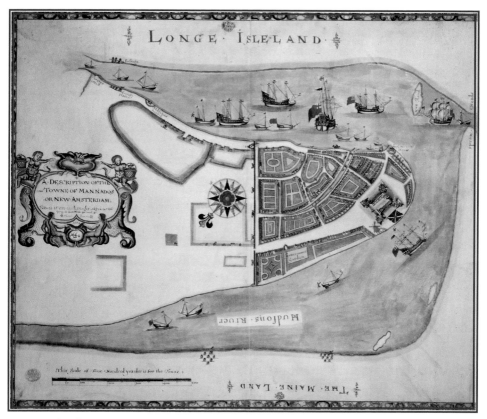

The first Europeans to explore the New World traded amicably with the local Native Americans in exchange for navigation, protection, and peace.

As Europeans began to settle in America, their presence encroached on the native peoples' way of life. The Iroquois eventually engaged in battles with them.

Mahicans in order to seize trade goods. Moreover, they tried to push out the Mahicans so they could dominate trade with the Dutch.

During this time the Iroquois engaged in their first battles with Europeans, and these fights set the stage for conflicts that later sorely tested the bonds of the confederacy. The first battle erupted in July of 1609 on the southern shore of Lake Champlain. Iroquois war parties had been raiding Algonquins, Montagnais, and Hurons, disrupting French trade. Samuel de Champlain (for whom the lake is named) led French forces, along with native warriors, against a band of Iroquois. Wearing metal armor and wielding muskets, the French overpowered the Iroquois, who wore wooden armor and fought with arrows. The following year, the French routed the Iroquois again, driving back their raiding parties. After this, the French became close allies of the Canadian Indians and frequently battled the Iroquois.

Frustrated in the north, the Iroquois turned eastward, where the Dutch traded. Besides raids and battles in Mahican territory, the Iroquois pushed farther east to attack the Abenaki in Maine. To the south, they attacked tribes in southern New England. With each advance into new territory, they traded with the French, Dutch, or English settlers there. In 1643, the Mohawk Nation negotiated a treaty with the Dutch. From the Dutch the Mohawks obtained firearms. Gradually the Dutch became friendly with the other tribes of the Iroquois Confederacy, and the two governments remained friendly throughout the Dutch occupation of that region. Then the British conquered the Dutch colony of New Netherlands, naming it New York, and they kept up the peace with the Iroquois.

The Iroquois Population Plummets

For the Iroquois, the seventeenth and eighteenth centuries were a time of almost continual warfare. Using new metal weapons and armor, they

When Samuel de Champlain found his exploration and trade disrupted by the Iroquois, he led French forces on an attack against them. The French and Iroquois would battle frequently.

continued to carry on warfare. In 1645 the Mohawk negotiated a peace treaty with the French and their Canadian Indian allies, but the peace lasted only a couple of years. Soon the Mohawk were again on the warpath to the north and encouraged their Iroquois allies to attack there as well. The power of the Iroquois Confederacy grew.

The Iroquois Constitution provided for the adoption of individuals from outside the member nations. Any member of the confederacy may propose the adoption of an individual, a family, or a group of families. The adoption is then reviewed and confirmed by the council lords. During times of warfare the Iroquois helped their numbers grow by adopting captives. An adoptee became a true member of his or her new family, sharing their identity and clan. Adoption also conferred Iroquois citizenship on a foreigner, and in a naming ceremony the adoptee received an Iroquois name. When European diseases began killing large numbers of Indians in the seventeenth century, the Iroquois often made raids and fought battles especially to take captives for adoption. In this way they could help keep their numbers from plummeting.

As the 1600s advanced, the Iroquois became increasingly embroiled in warfare with the French and their Indian allies to the north and west of Iroquois territory. Until 1701, bloody warfare alternated with short periods of peace and trade, usually negotiated by individual nations rather than the confederacy as a whole. In King William's War (1689–1697) many Iroquois, especially the Mohawk, Oneida, and Onondaga, fought fiercely against the French and their Indian allies. In this war France and Great Britain struggled for control of territory in the region of modern Nova Scotia, Quebec, and New England. In the 1690s alone, the Iroquois lost approximately 1,600 to 2,000 warriors in battle. They could not sustain their numbers, much less their power, if the pattern of loss continued.

Consequently, in 1701 the Iroquois Confederacy negotiated separate peace treaties with France and Great Britain. Until the middle of the century, the Iroquois generally maintained their neutrality with the French and the English. They began recovering from losses suffered during years of warfare. Also during this time, in 1722, the Tuscarora were admitted into the Iroquois league, thereafter known as the Six Nations Confederacy.

Conflict between Britain and France over control of the North American continent escalated. For two-thirds of a century, the Iroquois Confederacy carefully maintained neutrality toward France and Great Britain as the two European nations clashed in Queen Anne's War (1702–1713), King George's War (1744–1748), and the French and Indian War (1754–1763). Within the separate Iroquois nations, however, differences of opinion arose regarding which European power to support, and occasionally factions of Iroquois fought with one side or the other. In 1754, the year the French and Indian War began, the English invited Iroquois chiefs to the Albany Congress, where they asked the confederacy to side against the French. But the Iroquois persisted in their official neutrality toward both European powers.

While the league worked to maintain its neutrality toward the European powers, it felt no obligation to keep the peace with Indians to the south. For more than fifty years, the Iroquois warred against the Catawbas, the Cherokees, and others. The Iroquois Confederacy grew in political strength and power. After the English won the French and Indian War, though, the political landscape began to change. French colonies were taken over by the victorious English. Now the Iroquois found the English to be more demanding, for they no longer had to fear that the Iroquois would side with the French.

The American Revolution and a Threat to the Confederacy

Furthermore, the English colonies were now moving rapidly toward separation from Great Britain. After the French and Indian War, the British colonies turned their attention toward their dissatisfaction with British rule, taxation, and other issues. They staged protests such as the Boston Tea Party, in which colonists dressed as Mohawk Indians boarded English merchant ships and dumped cargoes of tea into the harbor. Then in 1775 war broke out between the British and the colonists, and in 1776 the colonies officially separated from England with the Declaration of Independence.

During the American Revolution (1775–1783) the Iroquois Confederacy faced a tremendous challenge. Until now the confederacy as a whole had not become involved in European conflicts and had maintained its policy of neutrality. But with the outbreak of the American Revolution neutrality was impossible. Each of the six Iroquois nations eventually chose to support either Britain or the United States. Siding with the British were four tribes: the Mohawk, Onondaga, Cayuga, and

Seneca. The Oneida and the Tuscarora sided with the Americans. Now Iroquois were pitted against Iroquois in battle for the first time since the Great Peace.

The American Revolution ended when, in Paris in 1783, the British signed a peace treaty with the United States, recognizing their independence. The Iroquois nations who had fought alongside either the British or the Americans were not included in the treaty. Consequently, Iroquois allies of the British feared retaliation from the victorious Americans. When General Frederick Haldimand, commander of British forces in Canada, proposed a solution, the tribes agreed. The British government bought a tract of land from the Mississauga Indians in Ontario, along the Grand River, and granted the land to Iroquois British Loyalists. Iroquois from all six tribes migrated to the Grand River Reservation, known today as the Six Nations Reserve.

The Confederacy and the United States

The era of greatness for the Six Nations Confederacy ended after the American Revolution, but the league did not disband. Today the Mohawk, Oneida, Onondaga, Cayuga, Seneca, and Tuscarora all remain members of the confederacy. However, they no longer live together in a wide swath of

Members of the Six Nations now live in upstate New York, Wisconsin, Oklahoma, and Canada. This Indian Pow Wow took place on a Six Nations Reserve in Onandaga, Ontario.

territory between the Genesee and Hudson Rivers in New York State. Instead, families and clans live on reservations in Ontario and Quebec in Canada, and in New York, Wisconsin, and Oklahoma in the United States.

The Onondaga, most of whom live just south of Syracuse, New York, remain the keepers of the council fire and host meetings of the Grand Council as in days of old. Because of the difficulty of traveling frequently to New York, the Iroquois in Canada established their own council fire on the

Grand River Reservation. For special occasions, that council joins the Grand Council at Onondaga in New York. For the most part, though, the Grand River council carries out governmental business with the Canadian government, and the Onondaga council in New York works with the United States government.

After the American Revolution, the exchange of ideas between the Iroquois and citizens of the United States gradually resumed. The Iroquois Constitution's provisions for female citizens became a subject of study and writing. Iroquois law protects specific rights of women in government and society, guaranteeing them equal participation in democratic processes. Women clan leaders are the legal guardians of the titles of the confederate lords, holding the power to nominate lords and to reprimand and remove errant lords from the council. In contrast, the US Constitution denied voting rights to women until 1920, when the Nineteenth Amendment was ratified.

The Iroquois Constitution's democratic provisions for women in the confederacy reflected traditional Iroquois roles of women in society. Women owned the land and controlled the stores of food, including game and fish brought home by men. Profits from the sale or trade of furs and skins were paid to the wife. Women had a voice in treaties, war decisions, and the sale of lands. In personal relationships a woman had protection from violence and abuse. Her family, particularly her brothers, were duty-bound to protect or separate her from an abusive spouse. In the case of separation or divorce, she had the right to all the possessions she brought to the union and to custody of the children.

In contrast, female citizens of the United States in the 1800s had no vote and certainly no say in war decisions or treaty negotiations. An unmarried woman could own property and control her earnings, but a married woman had no property rights, no control of the income she might earn, no protection from spousal abuse, and no child custody rights.

The political and social status of women in Iroquois and other Indian societies prompted early supporters of women's rights in the United States to study Iroquois society as a model of equality. Founders of the women's movement in the nineteenth century included Elizabeth Cady Stanton, Matilda Joslyn Gage, and Susan B. Anthony. These women and others studied, spoke, and wrote about the rights and liberties of Iroquois women. In an article in the *New York Evening Post* in 1875, Gage wrote that "division of power between the sexes in this Indian republic was nearly equal."[4] Other writers also noted the equality inherent in Iroquois society. Political theorist Friedrich Engels, writing in the late 1800s, observed that in Iroquois culture "All are free and equal—including the women."[5] The equality that Iroquois women hold under the Iroquois Constitution inspires modern-day women's rights leaders as well. Gloria Steinem said in an interview in the *San Francisco Chronicle* in 1998, "The Iroquois guaranteed the social and political power of women to such an extent that suffragists . . . who talked and to women from nearby tribes, were able to imagine a life of equality they had never known."[6]

The Iroquois Confederacy was not the only union of Native American nations. However, it was the most successful, because it was better established and more thoughtfully organized and executed. Although the Iroquois Confederacy did not survive as the power it once was, it served an important role in US history. While no one can be sure if the Iroquois Constitution influenced the US Constitution, it is certain that its democratic ideas and civic principles are thoroughly American.

THE GREAT BINDING LAW, GAYANASHAGOWA

1. I am Dekanawidah and with the Five Nations'
    Confederate Lords I plant the Tree of Great Peace.
    I plant it in your territory, Adodarhoh, and the
    Onondaga Nation, in the territory of you who are
    Fire Keepers.

    I name the tree the Tree of the Great Long
    Leaves. Under the shade of this Tree of the Great
    Peace we spread the soft white feathery down of the
    globe thistle as seats for you, Adodarhoh, and your
    cousin Lords.

    We place you upon those seats, spread soft
    with the feathery down of the globe thistle, there
    beneath the shade of the spreading branches of
    the Tree of Peace. There shall you sit and watch
    the Council Fire of the Confederacy of the Five
    Nations, and all the affairs of the Five Nations shall
    be transacted at this place before you, Adodarhoh,
    and your cousin Lords, by the Confederate Lords
    of the Five Nations.

2. Roots have spread out from the Tree of the Great
    Peace, one to the north, one to the east, one to the
    south and one to the west. The name of these roots

is The Great White Roots and their nature is Peace and Strength.

If any man or any nation outside the Five Nations shall obey the laws of the Great Peace and make known their disposition to the Lords of the Confederacy, they may trace the Roots to the Tree and if their minds are clean and they are obedient and promise to obey the wishes of the Confederate Council, they shall be welcomed to take shelter beneath the Tree of the Long Leaves.

We place at the top of the Tree of the Long Leaves an Eagle who is able to see afar. If he sees in the distance any evil approaching or any danger threatening he will at once warn the people of the Confederacy.

3.   To you Adodarhoh, the Onondaga cousin Lords, I and the other Confederate Lords have entrusted the caretaking and the watching of the Five Nations Council Fire.

When there is any business to be transacted and the Confederate Council is not in session, a messenger shall be dispatched either to Adodarhoh, Hononwirehtonh or Skanawatih, Fire Keepers, or to their War Chiefs with a full statement of the case desired to be considered. Then shall Adodarhoh call his cousin (associate) Lords together and consider whether or not the case is of sufficient importance to demand the attention of the Confederate Council. If so, Adodarhoh shall dispatch messengers to summon all the Confederate Lords to assemble beneath the Tree of the Long Leaves.

When the Lords are assembled the Council Fire shall be kindled, but not with chestnut wood, and Adodarhoh shall formally open the Council.

Then shall Adodarhoh and his cousin Lords, the Fire Keepers, announce the subject for discussion.

The Smoke of the Confederate Council Fire shall ever ascend and pierce the sky so that other nations who may be allies may see the Council Fire of the Great Peace.

Adodarhoh and his cousin Lords are entrusted with the Keeping of the Council Fire.

4. You, Adodarhoh, and your thirteen cousin Lords, shall faithfully keep the space about the Council Fire clean and you shall allow neither dust nor dirt to accumulate. I lay a Long Wing before you as a broom. As a weapon against a crawling creature I lay a staff with you so that you may thrust it away from the Council Fire. If you fail to cast it out then call the rest of the United Lords to your aid.

5. The Council of the Mohawk shall be divided into three parties as follows: Tekarihoken, Ayonhwhathah and Shadekariwade are the first party; Sharenhowaneh, Deyoenhegwenh and Oghrenghrehgowah are the second party, and Dehennakrineh, Aghstawenserenthah and Shoskoharowaneh are the third party. The third party is to listen only to the discussion of the first and second parties and if an error is made or the

proceeding is irregular they are to call attention to it, and when the case is right and properly decided by the two parties they shall confirm the decision of the two parties and refer the case to the Seneca Lords for their decision. When the Seneca Lords have decided in accord with the Mohawk Lords, the case or question shall be referred to the Cayuga and Oneida Lords on the opposite side of the house.

6. I, Dekanawidah, appoint the Mohawk Lords the heads and the leaders of the Five Nations Confederacy. The Mohawk Lords are the foundation of the Great Peace and it shall, therefore, be against the Great Binding Law to pass measures in the Confederate Council after the Mohawk Lords have protested against them.

    No council of the Confederate Lords shall be legal unless all the Mohawk Lords are present.

7. Whenever the Confederate Lords shall assemble for the purpose of holding a council, the Onondaga Lords shall open it by expressing their gratitude to their cousin Lords and greeting them, and they shall make an address and offer thanks to the earth where men dwell, to the streams of water, the pools, the springs and the lakes, to the maize and the fruits, to the medicinal herbs and trees, to the forest trees for their usefulness, to the animals that serve as food and give their pelts for clothing, to the great winds and the lesser winds, to the Thunderers, to the Sun, the mighty warrior, to the moon, to the messengers of the Creator who reveal his wishes

and to the Great Creator who dwells in the heavens above, who gives all the things useful to men, and who is the source and the ruler of health and life.

Then shall the Onondaga Lords declare the council open.

The council shall not sit after darkness has set in.

8. The Fire Keepers shall formally open and close all councils of the Confederate Lords, and they shall pass upon all matters deliberated upon by the two sides and render their decision.

Every Onondaga Lord (or his deputy) must be present at every Confederate Council and must agree with the majority without unwarrantable dissent, so that a unanimous decision may be rendered.

If Adodarhoh or any of his cousin Lords are absent from a Confederate Council, any other Fire Keeper may open and close the Council, but the Fire Keepers present may not give any decisions, unless the matter is of small importance.

9. All the business of the Five Nations Confederate Council shall be conducted by the two combined bodies of Confederate Lords. First the question shall be passed upon by the Mohawk and Seneca Lords, then it shall be discussed and passed by the Oneida and Cayuga Lords. Their decisions shall then be referred to the Onondaga Lords, (Fire Keepers) for final judgment.

The same process shall obtain when a question is brought before the council by an individual or a War Chief.

10.   In all cases the procedure must be as follows: when the Mohawk and Seneca Lords have unanimously agreed upon a question, they shall report their decision to the Cayuga and Oneida Lords who shall deliberate upon the question and report a unanimous decision to the Mohawk Lords. The Mohawk Lords will then report the standing of the case to the Fire Keepers, who shall render a decision as they see fit in case of a disagreement by the two bodies, or confirm the decisions of the two bodies if they are identical. The Fire Keepers shall then report their decision to the Mohawk Lords who shall announce it to the open council.

11.   If through any misunderstanding or obstinacy on the part of the Fire Keepers, they render a decision at variance with that of the Two Sides, the Two Sides shall reconsider the matter and if their decisions are jointly the same as before they shall report to the Fire Keepers who are then compelled to confirm their joint decision.

12.   When a case comes before the Onondaga Lords (Fire Keepers) for discussion and decision, Adodarho shall introduce the matter to his comrade Lords who shall then discuss it in their two bodies. Every Onondaga Lord except Hononwiretonh shall deliberate and he shall listen only. When a

unanimous decision shall have been reached by the two bodies of Fire Keepers, Adodarho shall notify Hononwiretonh of the fact when he shall confirm it. He shall refuse to confirm a decision if it is not unanimously agreed upon by both sides of the Fire Keepers.

13. No Lord shall ask a question of the body of Confederate Lords when they are discussing a case, question or proposition. He may only deliberate in a low tone with the separate body of which he is a member.

14. When the Council of the Five Nation Lords shall convene they shall appoint a speaker for the day. He shall be a Lord of either the Mohawk, Onondaga or Seneca Nation.

    The next day the Council shall appoint another speaker, but the first speaker may be reappointed if there is no objection, but a speaker's term shall not be regarded more than for the day.

15. No individual or foreign nation interested in a case, question or proposition shall have any voice in the Confederate Council except to answer a question put to him or them by the speaker for the Lords.

16. If the conditions which shall arise at any future time call for an addition to or change of this law, the case shall be carefully considered and if a new beam seems necessary or beneficial, the proposed change shall be voted upon and if adopted it shall be called, "Added to the Rafters."

17. A bunch of a certain number of shell (wampum) strings each two spans in length shall be given to each of the female families in which the Lordship titles are vested. The right of bestowing the title shall be hereditary in the family of the females legally possessing the bunch of shell strings and the strings shall be the token that the females of the family have the proprietary right to the Lordship title for all time to come, subject to certain restrictions hereinafter mentioned.

18. If any Confederate Lord neglects or refuses to attend the Confederate Council, the other Lords of the Nation of which he is a member shall require their War Chief to request the female sponsors of the Lord so guilty of defection to demand his attendance of the Council. If he refuses, the women holding the title shall immediately select another candidate for the title.

    No Lord shall be asked more than once to attend the Confederate Council.

19. If at any time it shall be manifest that a Confederate Lord has not in mind the welfare of the people or disobeys the rules of this Great Law, the men or women of the Confederacy, or both jointly, shall come to the Council and upbraid the erring Lord through his War Chief. If the complaint of the people through the War Chief is not heeded the first time it shall be uttered again and then if no attention is given a third complaint and warning shall be given. If the Lord is contumacious, the matter shall

go to the council of War Chiefs. The War Chiefs shall then divest the erring Lord of his title by order of the women in whom the titleship is vested. When the Lord is deposed the women shall notify the Confederate Lords through their War Chief, and the Confederate Lords shall sanction the act. The women will then select another of their sons as a candidate and the Lords shall elect him. Then shall the chosen one be installed by the Installation Ceremony. When a Lord is to be deposed, his War Chief shall address him as follows:

"So you,_____, disregard and set at naught the warnings of your women relatives. So you fling the warnings over your shoulder to cast them behind you.

"Behold the brightness of the Sun and in the brightness of the Sun's light I depose you of your title and remove the sacred emblem of your Lordship title. I remove from your brow the deer's antlers, which was the emblem of your position and token of your nobility. I now depose you and return the antlers to the women whose heritage they are."

The War Chief shall now address the women of the deposed Lord and say:

"Mothers, as I have now deposed your Lord, I now return to you the emblem and the title of Lordship, therefore repossess them."

Again addressing himself to the deposed Lord he shall say:

"As I have now deposed and discharged you so you are now no longer Lord. You shall now go your way alone, the rest of the people of the Confederacy will not go with you, for we know not the kind of mind that possesses you. As the Creator has nothing to do with wrong so he will not come to rescue you from the precipice of destruction in which you have cast yourself. You shall never be restored to the position which you once occupied."

Then shall the War Chief address himself to the Lords of the Nation to which the deposed Lord belongs and say:

"Know you, my Lords, that I have taken the deer's antlers from the brow of _____, the emblem of his position and token of his greatness."

The Lords of the Confederacy shall then have no other alternative than to sanction the discharge of the offending Lord.

20. If a Lord of the Confederacy of the Five Nations should commit murder the other Lords of the Nation shall assemble at the place where the corpse lies and prepare to depose the criminal Lord. If it is impossible to meet at the scene of the crime the Lords shall discuss the matter at the next Council of their Nation and request their War Chief to depose the Lord guilty of crime, to "bury" his women relatives and to transfer the Lordship title to a sister family.

The War Chief shall address the Lord guilty of murder and say:

"So you, _____ (giving his name) did kill _____ (naming the slain man), with your own hands! You have committed a grave sin in the eyes of the Creator. Behold the bright light of the Sun, and in the brightness of the Sun's light I depose you of your title and remove the horns, the sacred emblems of your Lordship title. I remove from your brow the deer's antlers, which was the emblem of your position and token of your nobility. I now depose you and expel you and you shall depart at once from the territory of the Five Nations Confederacy and nevermore return again. We, the Five Nations Confederacy, moreover, bury your women relatives because the ancient Lordship title was never intended to have any union with bloodshed. Henceforth it shall not be their heritage. By the evil deed that you have done they have forfeited it forever."

The War Chief shall then hand the title to a sister family and he shall address it and say:

"Our mothers, _____, listen attentively while I address you on a solemn and important subject. I hereby transfer to you an ancient Lordship title for a great calamity has befallen it in the hands of the family of a former Lord. We trust that you, our mothers, will always guard it, and that you will warn your Lord always to be dutiful and to advise his people to ever live in love, peace and harmony that a great calamity may never happen again."

21. Certain physical defects in a Confederate Lord make him ineligible to sit in the Confederate Council.

Such defects are infancy, idiocy, blindness, deafness, dumbness and impotency. When a Confederate Lord is restricted by any of these conditions, a deputy shall be appointed by his sponsors to act for him, but in case of extreme necessity the restricted Lord may exercise his rights.

22. If a Confederate Lord desires to resign his title he shall notify the Lords of the Nation of which he is a member of his intention. If his coactive Lords refuse to accept his resignation he may not resign his title. A Lord in proposing to resign may recommend any proper candidate which recommendation shall be received by the Lords, but unless confirmed and nominated by the women who hold the title the candidate so named shall not be considered.

23. Any Lord of the Five Nations Confederacy may construct shell strings (or wampum belts) of any size or length as pledges or records of matters of national or international importance.

    When it is necessary to dispatch a shell string by a War Chief or other messenger as the token of a summons, the messenger shall recite the contents of the string to the party to whom it is sent. That party shall repeat the message and return the shell string and if there has been a summons he shall make ready for the journey.

    Any of the people of the Five Nations may use shells (or wampum) as the record of a pledge, contract or an agreement entered into and the same shall be binding as soon as shell strings shall have been exchanged by both parties.

24. The Lords of the Confederacy of the Five Nations shall be mentors of the people for all time. The thickness of their skin shall be seven spans—which is to say that they shall be proof against anger, offensive actions and criticism. Their hearts shall be full of peace and good will and their minds filled with a yearning for the welfare of the people of the Confederacy. With endless patience they shall carry out their duty and their firmness shall be tempered with a tenderness for their people. Neither anger nor fury shall find lodgement in their minds and all their words and actions shall be marked by calm deliberation.

25. If a Lord of the Confederacy should seek to establish any authority independent of the jurisdiction of the Confederacy of the Great Peace, which is the Five Nations, he shall be warned three times in open council, first by the women relatives, second by the men relatives and finally by the Lords of the Confederacy of the Nation to which he belongs. If the offending Lord is still obdurate he shall be dismissed by the War Chief of his nation for refusing to conform to the laws of the Great Peace. His nation shall then install the candidate nominated by the female name holders of his family.

26. It shall be the duty of all of the Five Nations Confederate Lords, from time to time as occasion

demands, to act as mentors and spiritual guides of their people and remind them of their Creator's will and words. They shall say:

"Hearken, that peace may continue unto future days!

"Always listen to the words of the Great Creator, for he has spoken.

"United people, let not evil find lodging in your minds.

"For the Great Creator has spoken and the cause of Peace shall not become old.

"The cause of peace shall not die if you remember the Great Creator."

Every Confederate Lord shall speak words such as these to promote peace.

27.   All Lords of the Five Nations Confederacy must be honest in all things. They must not idle or gossip, but be men possessing those honorable qualities that make true royaneh. It shall be a serious wrong for anyone to lead a Lord into trivial affairs, for the people must ever hold their Lords high in estimation out of respect to their honorable positions.

28.   When a candidate Lord is to be installed8 he shall furnish four strings of shells (or wampum) one span in length bound together at one end. Such will constitute the evidence of his pledge to the Confederate Lords that he will live according to the constitution of the Great Peace and exercise justice in all affairs.

When the pledge is furnished the Speaker of the Council must hold the shell strings in his hand and address the opposite side of the Council Fire and he shall commence his address saying:

"Now behold him. He has now become a Confederate Lord. See how splendid he looks."

An address may then follow. At the end of it he shall send the bunch of shell strings to the opposite side and they shall be received as evidence of the pledge. Then shall the opposite side say:

"We now do crown you with the sacred emblem of the deer's antlers, the emblem of your Lordship. You shall now become a mentor of the people of the Five Nations. The thickness of your skin shall be seven spans—which is to say that you shall be proof against anger, offensive actions and criticism. Your heart shall be filled with peace and good will and your mind filled with a yearning for the welfare of the people of the Confederacy. With endless patience you shall carry out your duty and your firmness shall be tempered with tenderness for your people. Neither anger nor fury shall find lodgement in your mind and all your words and actions shall be marked with calm deliberation. In all of your deliberations in the Confederate Council, in your efforts at law making, in all your official acts, self interest shall be cast into oblivion. Cast not over your shoulder behind you the warnings of the nephews and nieces should they chide you for any error or wrong you may do, but return to the way of the Great Law which is just and right. Look and listen for the welfare of the whole people and have always in view not only the present but also the coming generations, even those whose faces are yet beneath the surface of the ground—the unborn of the future Nation."

29. When a Lordship title is to be conferred, the candidate Lord shall furnish the cooked venison, the corn bread and the corn soup, together with other necessary things and the labor for the Conferring of Titles Festival.

30. The Lords of the Confederacy may confer the Lordship title upon a candidate whenever the Great Law is recited, if there be a candidate, for the Great Law speaks all the rules.

31. If a Lord of the Confederacy should become seriously ill and be thought near death, the women who are heirs of his title shall go to his house and lift his crown of deer antlers, the emblem of his Lordship, and place them at one side. If the Creator spares him and he rises from his bed of sickness he may rise with the antlers on his brow.

The following words shall be used to temporarily remove the antlers:

"Now our comrade Lord (or our relative Lord) the time has come when we must approach you in your illness. We remove for a time the deer's antlers from your brow, we remove the emblem of your Lordship title. The Great Law has decreed that no Lord should end his life with the antlers on his brow. We therefore lay them aside in the room. If the Creator spares you and you recover from your illness you shall rise from your bed with the antlers on your brow as before and you shall resume your duties as Lord of the Confederacy and you may labor again for the Confederate people."

32. If a Lord of the Confederacy should die while the Council of the Five Nations is in session the Council shall adjourn for ten days. No Confederate Council shall sit within ten days of the death of a Lord of the Confederacy.

If the Three Brothers (the Mohawk, the Onondaga and the Seneca) should lose one of their Lords by death, the Younger Brothers (the Oneida and the Cayuga) shall come to the surviving Lords of the Three Brothers on the tenth day and console them. If the Younger Brothers lose one of their Lords then the Three Brothers shall come to them and console them. And the consolation shall be the reading of the contents of the thirteen shell (wampum) strings of Ayonhwhathah. At the termination of this rite a successor shall be appointed, to be appointed by the women heirs of the Lordship title. If the women are not yet ready to place their nominee before the Lords the Speaker shall say, "Come let us go out."

All shall leave the Council or the place of gathering. The installation shall then wait until such a time as the women are ready. The Speaker shall lead the way from the house by saying, "Let us depart to the edge of the woods and lie in waiting on our bellies."

When the women title holders shall have chosen one of their sons the Confederate Lords will assemble in two places, the Younger Brothers in one place and the Three Older Brothers in another. The Lords who are to console the mourning Lords shall choose one of their number to sing the Pacification Hymn as they journey to the sorrowing Lords. The singer shall lead the way and the Lords and the people shall follow. When they reach the sorrowing Lords they shall hail the candidate Lord and perform the rite of Conferring the Lordship Title.

33.　When a Confederate Lord dies, the surviving relatives shall immediately dispatch a messenger, a member of another clan, to the Lords in another locality. When the runner comes within hailing distance of the locality he shall utter a sad wail, thus: "Kwa-ah, Kwa-ah, Kwa-ah!"

The sound shall be repeated three times and then again and again at intervals as many times as the distance may require. When the runner arrives at the settlement the people shall assemble and one must ask him the nature of his sad message. He shall then say, "Let us consider."

Then he shall tell them of the death of the Lord. He shall deliver to them a string of shells (wampum) and say "Here is the testimony, you have heard the message."

He may then return home. It now becomes the duty of the Lords of the locality to send runners to other localities and each locality shall send other messengers until all Lords are notified. Runners shall travel day and night.

34. If a Lord dies and there is no candidate qualified for the office in the family of the women title holders, the Lords of the Nation shall give the title into the hands of a sister family in the clan until such a time as the original family produces a candidate, when the title shall be restored to the rightful owners.

    No Lordship title may be carried into the grave. The Lords of the Confederacy may dispossess a dead Lord of his title even at the grave.

35. Should any man of the Nation assist with special ability or show great interest in the affairs of the Nation, if he proves himself wise, honest and worthy of confidence, the Confederate Lords may elect him to a seat with them and he may sit in the Confederate Council. He shall be proclaimed a "Pine Tree sprung up for the Nation" and shall be installed as such at the next assembly for the installation of Lords. Should he ever do anything contrary to the rules of the Great Peace, he may not be deposed from office—no one shall cut him down—but thereafter everyone shall be deaf to his voice and his advice. Should he resign his seat and title no one shall prevent him. A Pine Tree chief has no authority to name a successor nor is his title hereditary.

36. The title names of the Chief Confederate Lords' War Chiefs shall be:

    Ayonwaehs, War Chief under Lord Takarihoken (Mohawk)

    Kahonwahdironh, War Chief under Lord Odatshedeh (Oneida)

    Ayendes, War Chief under Lord Adodarhoh (Onondaga)

    Wenenhs, War Chief under Lord Dekaenyonh (Cayuga)

    Shoneradowaneh, War Chief under Lord Skanyadariyo (Seneca)

    The women heirs of each head Lord's title shall be the heirs of the War Chief's title of their respective Lord.

    The War Chiefs shall be selected from the eligible sons of the female families holding the head Lordship titles.

37. There shall be one War Chief for each Nation and their duties shall be to carry messages for their Lords and to take up the arms of war in case of emergency. They shall not participate in the proceedings of the Confederate Council but shall watch its progress and in case of an erroneous action by a Lord they shall receive the complaints of the people and convey the warnings of the women to him. The people who wish to convey messages to the Lords in the Confederate Council shall do so through the War Chief of their Nation. It shall ever be his duty

to lay the cases, questions and propositions of the people before the Confederate Council.

38. When a War Chief dies another shall be installed by the same rite as that by which a Lord is installed.

39. If a War Chief acts contrary to instructions or against the provisions of the Laws of the Great Peace, doing so in the capacity of his office, he shall be deposed by his women relatives and by his men relatives. Either the women or the men alone or jointly may act in such a case. The women title holders shall then choose another candidate.

40. When the Lords of the Confederacy take occasion to dispatch a messenger in behalf of the Confederate Council, they shall wrap up any matter they may send and instruct the messenger to remember his errand, to turn not aside but to proceed faithfully to his destination and deliver his message according to every instruction.

41. If a message borne by a runner is the warning of an invasion he shall whoop, "Kwa-ah, Kwa-ah," twice and repeat at short intervals; then again at a longer interval.

    If a human being is found dead, the finder shall not touch the body but return home immediately shouting at short intervals, "Koo-weh!"

42. Among the Five Nations and their posterity there shall be the following original clans: Great Name Bearer, Ancient Name Bearer, Great Bear, Ancient

Bear, Turtle, Painted Turtle, Standing Rock, Large Plover, Deer, Pigeon Hawk, Eel, Ball, Opposite-Side-of-the-Hand, and Wild Potatoes. These clans distributed through their respective Nations, shall be the sole owners and holders of the soil of the country and in them is it vested as a birthright.

43. People of the Five Nations members of a certain clan shall recognize every other member of that clan, irrespective of the Nation, as relatives. Men and women, therefore, members of the same clan are forbidden to marry.

44. The lineal descent of the people of the Five Nations shall run in the female line. Women shall be considered the progenitors of the Nation. They shall own the land and the soil. Men and women shall follow the status of the mother.

45. The women heirs of the Confederated Lordship titles shall be called Royaneh (Noble) for all time to come.

46. The women of the Forty Eight (now fifty) Royaneh families shall be the heirs of the Authorized Names for all time to come.

    When an infant of the Five Nations is given an Authorized Name at the Midwinter Festival or at the Ripe Corn Festival, one in the cousinhood of which the infant is a member shall be appointed a speaker. He shall then announce to the opposite cousinhood the names of the father and the mother of the child together with the clan of the mother.

Then the speaker shall announce the child's name twice. The uncle of the child shall then take the child in his arms and walking up and down the room shall sing: "My head is firm, I am of the Confederacy."

As he sings, the opposite cousinhood shall respond by chanting, "Hyenh, Hyenh, Hyenh, Hyenh," until the song is ended.

47. If the female heirs of a Confederate Lord's title become extinct, the title right shall be given by the Lords of the Confederacy to the sister family whom they shall elect and that family shall hold the name and transmit it to their (female) heirs, but they shall not appoint any of their sons as a candidate for a title until all the eligible men of the former family shall have died or otherwise have become ineligible.

48. If all the heirs of a Lordship title become extinct, and all the families in the clan, then the title shall be given by the Lords of the Confederacy to the family in a sister clan whom they shall elect.

49. If any of the Royaneh women, heirs of a titleship, shall wilfully withhold a Lordship or other title and refuse to bestow it, or if such heirs abandon, forsake or despise their heritage, then shall such women be deemed buried and their family extinct. The titleship shall then revert to a sister family or clan upon application and complaint. The Lords of the Confederacy shall elect the family or clan which shall in future hold the title.

50. The Royaneh women of the Confederacy heirs of the Lordship titles shall elect two women of their family as cooks for the Lord when the people shall assemble at his house for business or other purposes.

    It is not good nor honorable for a Confederate Lord to allow his people whom he has called to go hungry.

51. When a Lord holds a conference in his home, his wife, if she wishes, may prepare the food for the Union Lords who assemble with him. This is an honorable right which she may exercise and an expression of her esteem.

52. The Royaneh women, heirs of the Lordship titles, shall, should it be necessary, correct and admonish the holders of their titles. Those only who attend the Council may do this and those who do not shall not object to what has been said nor strive to undo the action.

53. When the Royaneh women, holders of a Lordship title, select one of their sons as a candidate, they shall select one who is trustworthy, of good character, of honest disposition, one who manages his own affairs, supports his own family, if any, and who has proven a faithful man to his Nation.

54. When a Lordship title becomes vacant through death or other cause, the Royaneh women of the clan in which the title is hereditary shall hold a council and shall choose one from among their

sons to fill the office made vacant. Such a candidate shall not be the father of any Confederate Lord. If the choice is unanimous the name is referred to the men relatives of the clan. If they should disapprove it shall be their duty to select a candidate from among their own number. If then the men and women are unable to decide which of the two candidates shall be named, then the matter shall be referred to the Confederate Lords in the Clan. They shall decide which candidate shall be named. If the men and the women agree to a candidate his name shall be referred to the sister clans for confirmation. If the sister clans confirm the choice, they shall refer their action to their Confederate Lords who shall ratify the choice and present it to their cousin Lords, and if the cousin Lords confirm the name then the candidate shall be installed by the proper ceremony for the conferring of Lordship titles.

55.　A large bunch of shell strings, in the making of which the Five Nations Confederate Lords have equally contributed, shall symbolize the completeness of the union and certify the pledge of the nations represented by the Confederate Lords of the Mohawk, the Oneida, the Onondaga, the Cayuga and the Seneca, that all are united and formed into one body or union called the Union of the Great Law, which they have established.

　　A bunch of shell strings is to be the symbol of the council fire of the Five Nations Confederacy. And the Lord whom the council of Fire Keepers shall appoint to speak for them in opening the council shall hold the strands of shells in his hands when speaking. When he finishes speaking he shall deposit the strings on an elevated place (or pole) so that all the assembled Lords and the people may see it and know that the council is open and in progress.

When the council adjourns the Lord who has been appointed by his comrade Lords to close it shall take the strands of shells in his hands and address the assembled Lords. Thus will the council adjourn until such time and place as appointed by the council. Then shall the shell strings be placed in a place for safekeeping.

Every five years the Five Nations Confederate Lords and the people shall assemble together and shall ask one another if their minds are still in the same spirit of unity for the Great Binding Law and if any of the Five Nations shall not pledge continuance and steadfastness to the pledge of unity then the Great Binding Law shall dissolve.

56. Five strings of shell tied together as one shall represent the Five Nations. Each string shall represent one territory and the whole a completely united territory known as the Five Nations Confederate territory.

57. Five arrows shall be bound together very strong and each arrow shall represent one nation. As the five arrows are strongly bound this shall symbolize the complete union of the nations. Thus are the Five

Nations united completely and enfolded together, united into one head, one body and one mind. Therefore they shall labor, legislate and council together for the interest of future generations.

The Lords of the Confederacy shall eat together from one bowl the feast of cooked beaver's tail. While they are eating they are to use no sharp utensils for if they should they might accidentally cut one another and bloodshed would follow. All measures must be taken to prevent the spilling of blood in any way.

58. There are now the Five Nations Confederate Lords standing with joined hands in a circle. This signifies and provides that should any one of the Confederate Lords leave the council and this Confederacy his crown of deer's horns, the emblem of his Lordship title, together with his birthright, shall lodge on the arms of the Union Lords whose hands are so joined. He forfeits his title and the crown falls from his brow but it shall remain in the Confederacy.

A further meaning of this is that if any time any one of the Confederate Lords choose to submit to the law of a foreign people he is no longer in but out of the Confederacy, and persons of this class shall be called "They have alienated themselves." Likewise such persons who submit to laws of foreign nations shall forfeit all birthrights and claims on the Five Nations Confederacy and territory.

You, the Five Nations Confederate Lords, be firm so that if a tree falls on your joined arms it shall not separate or weaken your hold. So shall the strength of the union be preserved.

59. A bunch of wampum shells on strings, three spans of the hand in length, the upper half of the bunch being white and the lower half black, and formed from equal contributions of the men of the Five Nations, shall be a token that the men have combined themselves into one head, one body and one thought, and it shall also symbolize their ratification of the peace pact of the Confederacy, whereby the Lords of the Five Nations have established the Great Peace.

The white portion of the shell strings represent the women and the black portion the men. The black portion, furthermore, is a token of power and authority vested in the men of the Five Nations.

This string of wampum vests the people with the right to correct their erring Lords. In case a part or all the Lords pursue a course not vouched for by the people and heed not the third warning of their women relatives, then the matter shall be taken to the General Council of the women of the Five Nations. If the Lords notified and warned three times fail to heed, then the case falls into the hands of the men of the Five Nations. The War Chiefs shall then, by right of such power and authority, enter the open council to warn the Lord or Lords to return from the wrong course. If the Lords heed the warning they shall say, "we will reply tomorrow."

If then an answer is returned in favor of justice and in accord with this Great Law, then the Lords shall individually pledge themselves again by again furnishing the necessary shells for the pledge. Then shall the War Chief or Chiefs exhort the Lords urging them to be just and true.

Should it happen that the Lords refuse to heed the third warning, then two courses are open: either the men may decide in their council to depose the Lord or Lords or to club them to death with war clubs. Should they in their council decide to take the first course the War Chief shall address the Lord or Lords, saying: "Since you the Lords of the Five Nations have refused to return to the procedure of the Constitution, we now declare your seats vacant, we take off your horns, the token of your Lordship, and others shall be chosen and installed in your seats, therefore vacate your seats."

Should the men in their council adopt the second course, the War Chief shall order his men to enter the council, to take positions beside the Lords, sitting between them wherever possible. When this is accomplished the War Chief holding in his outstretched hand a bunch of black wampum strings shall say to the erring Lords: "So now, Lords of the Five United Nations, harken to these last words from your men. You have not heeded the warnings of the women relatives, you have not heeded the warnings of the General Council of women and you have not heeded the warnings of the men of the nations, all urging you to return to

the right course of action. Since you are determined
to resist and to withhold justice from your people
there is only one course for us to adopt."

At this point the War Chief shall let drop the
bunch of black wampum and the men shall spring
to their feet and club the erring Lords to death.
Any erring Lord may submit before the War Chief
lets fall the black wampum. Then his execution is
withheld.

The black wampum here used symbolizes that
the power to execute is buried but that it may be
raised up again by the men. It is buried but when
occasion arises they may pull it up and derive their
power and authority to act as here described.

60. A broad dark belt of wampum of thirty-eight rows,
having a white heart in the center, on either side of
which are two white squares all connected with the
heart by white rows of beads shall be the emblem of
the unity of the Five Nations.

The first of the squares on the left represents
the Mohawk nation and its territory; the second
square on the left and the one near the heart,
represents the Oneida nation and its territory; the
white heart in the middle represents the Onondaga
nation and its territory, and it also means that the
heart of the Five Nations is single in its loyalty
to the Great Peace, that the Great Peace is lodged
in the heart (meaning the Onondaga Lords), and
that the Council Fire is to burn there for the Five
Nations, and further, it means that the authority is

given to advance the cause of peace whereby hostile nations out of the Confederacy shall cease warfare; the white square to the right of the heart represents the Cayuga nation and its territory and the fourth and last white square represents the Seneca nation and its territory.

White shall here symbolize that no evil or jealous thoughts shall creep into the minds of the Lords while in Council under the Great Peace. White, the emblem of peace, love, charity and equity surrounds and guards the Five Nations.

61. Should a great calamity threaten the generations rising and living of the Five United Nations, then he who is able to climb to the top of the Tree of the Great Long Leaves may do so. When, then, he reaches the top of the tree he shall look about in all directions, and, should he see that evil things indeed are approaching, then he shall call to the people of the Five United Nations assembled beneath the Tree of the Great Long Leaves and say: "A calamity threatens your happiness."

Then shall the Lords convene in council and discuss the impending evil.

When all the truths relating to the trouble shall be fully known and found to be truths, then shall the people seek out a Tree of Ka-hon-ka-ah-go-nah, [a great swamp Elm], and when they shall find it they shall assemble their heads together and lodge for a time between its roots. Then, their labors being finished, they may hope for happiness for many days after.

62.   When the Confederate Council of the Five Nations declares for a reading of the belts of shell calling to mind these laws, they shall provide for the reader a specially made mat woven of the fibers of wild hemp. The mat shall not be used again, for such formality is called the honoring of the importance of the law.

63.   Should two sons of opposite sides of the council fire agree in a desire to hear the reciting of the laws of the Great Peace and so refresh their memories in the way ordained by the founder of the Confederacy, they shall notify Adodarho. He then shall consult with five of his coactive Lords and they in turn shall consult with their eight brethren. Then should they decide to accede to the request of the two sons from opposite sides of the Council Fire, Adodarho shall send messengers to notify the Chief Lords of each of the Five Nations. Then they shall despatch their War Chiefs to notify their brother and cousin Lords of the meeting and its time and place.

When all have come and have assembled, Adodarhoh, in conjunction with his cousin Lords, shall appoint one Lord who shall repeat the laws of the Great Peace. Then shall they announce who they have chosen to repeat the laws of the Great Peace to the two sons. Then shall the chosen one repeat the laws of the Great Peace.

64. At the ceremony of the installation of Lords if there is only one expert speaker and singer of the law and the Pacification Hymn to stand at the council fire, then when this speaker and singer has finished addressing one side of the fire he shall go to the opposite side and reply to his own speech and song. He shall thus act for both sides of the fire until the entire ceremony has been completed. Such a speaker and singer shall be termed the "Two Faced" because he speaks and sings for both sides of the fire.

65. I, Dekanawida, and the Union Lords, now uproot the tallest pine tree and into the cavity thereby made we cast all weapons of war. Into the depths of the earth, down into the deep under-earth currents of water flowing to unknown regions we cast all the weapons of strife. We bury them from sight and we plant again the tree. Thus shall the Great Peace be established and hostilities shall no longer be known between the Five Nations but peace to the United People.

66. The father of a child of great comeliness, learning, ability or specially loved because of some circumstance may, at the will of the child's clan, select a name from his own (the father's) clan and bestow it by ceremony, such as is provided. This naming shall be only temporary and shall be called, "A name hung about the neck."

67. Should any person, a member of the Five Nations' Confederacy, specially esteem a man or woman of another clan or of a foreign nation, he may choose a name and bestow it upon that person so esteemed. The naming shall be in accord with the ceremony of bestowing names. Such a name is only a temporary one and shall be called "A name hung about the neck." A short string of shells shall be delivered with the name as a record and a pledge.

68. Should any member of the Five Nations, a family or person belonging to a foreign nation submit a proposal for adoption into a clan of one of the Five Nations, he or they shall furnish a string of shells, a span in length, as a pledge to the clan into which he or they wish to be adopted. The Lords of the nation shall then consider the proposal and submit a decision.

69. Any member of the Five Nations who through esteem or other feeling wishes to adopt an individual, a family or number of families may offer adoption to him or them and if accepted the matter shall be brought to the attention of the Lords for confirmation and the Lords must confirm adoption.

70. When the adoption of anyone shall have been confirmed by the Lords of the Nation, the Lords shall address the people of their nation and say: "Now you of our nation, be informed that such a person, such a family or such families have ceased forever to bear their birth nation's name and have

buried it in the depths of the earth. Henceforth let no one of our nation ever mention the original name or nation of their birth. To do so will be to hasten the end of our peace.

71. When any person or family belonging to the Five Nations desires to abandon their birth nation and the territory of the Five Nations, they shall inform the Lords of their nation and the Confederate Council of the Five Nations shall take cognizance of it.

72. When any person or any of the people of the Five Nations emigrate and reside in a region distant from the territory of the Five Nations Confederacy, the Lords of the Five Nations at will may send a messenger carrying a broad belt of black shells and when the messenger arrives he shall call the people together or address them personally displaying the belt of shells and they shall know that this is an order for them to return to their original homes and to their council fires.

73. The soil of the earth from one end of the land to the other is the property of the people who inhabit it. By birthright the Ongwehonweh (Original beings) are the owners of the soil which they own and occupy and none other may hold it. The same law has been held from the oldest times.

　　The Great Creator has made us of the one blood and of the same soil he made us and as only different tongues constitute different nations he established different hunting grounds and territories and made boundary lines between them.

74.   When any alien nation or individual is admitted into the Five Nations the admission shall be understood only to be a temporary one. Should the person or nation create loss, do wrong or cause suffering of any kind to endanger the peace of the Confederacy, the Confederate Lords shall order one of their war chiefs to reprimand him or them and if a similar offense is again committed the offending party or parties shall be expelled from the territory of the Five United Nations.

75.   When a member of an alien nation comes to the territory of the Five Nations and seeks refuge and permanent residence, the Lords of the Nation to which he comes shall extend hospitality and make him a member of the nation. Then shall he be accorded equal rights and privileges in all matters except as after mentioned.

76.   No body of alien people who have been adopted temporarily shall have a vote in the council of the Lords of the Confederacy, for only they who have been invested with Lordship titles may vote in the Council. Aliens have nothing by blood to make claim to a vote and should they have it, not knowing all the traditions of the Confederacy, might go against its Great Peace. In this manner the Great Peace would be endangered and perhaps be destroyed.

77. When the Lords of the Confederacy decide to admit a foreign nation and an adoption is made, the Lords shall inform the adopted nation that its admission is only temporary. They shall also say to the nation that it must never try to control, to interfere with or to injure the Five Nations nor disregard the Great Peace or any of its rules or customs. That in no way should they cause disturbance or injury. Then should the adopted nation disregard these injunctions, their adoption shall be annulled and they shall be expelled.

The expulsion shall be in the following manner: The council shall appoint one of their War Chiefs to convey the message of annulment and he shall say, "You (naming the nation) listen to me while I speak. I am here to inform you again of the will of the Five Nations' Council. It was clearly made known to you at a former time. Now the Lords of the Five Nations have decided to expel you and cast you out. We disown you now and annul your adoption. Therefore you must look for a path in which to go and lead away all your people. It was you, not we, who committed wrong and caused this sentence of annulment. So then go your way and depart from the territory of the Five Nations and from the Confederacy."

78. Whenever a foreign nation enters the Confederacy or accepts the Great Peace, the Five Nations and the foreign nation shall enter into an agreement and compact by which the foreign nation shall

endeavor to persuade other nations to accept the Great Peace.

79. Skanawatih shall be vested with a double office, duty and with double authority. One-half of his being shall hold the Lordship title and the other half shall hold the title of War Chief. In the event of war he shall notify the five War Chiefs of the Confederacy and command them to prepare for war and have their men ready at the appointed time and place for engagement with the enemy of the Great Peace.

80. When the Confederate Council of the Five Nations has for its object the establishment of the Great Peace among the people of an outside nation and that nation refuses to accept the Great Peace, then by such refusal they bring a declaration of war upon themselves from the Five Nations. Then shall the Five Nations seek to establish the Great Peace by a conquest of the rebellious nation.

81. When the men of the Five Nations, now called forth to become warriors, are ready for battle with an obstinate opposing nation that has refused to accept the Great Peace, then one of the five War Chiefs shall be chosen by the warriors of the Five Nations to lead the army into battle. It shall be the duty of the War Chief so chosen to come before his warriors and address them. His aim shall be to impress upon them the necessity of good behavior and strict obedience to all the commands of the

War Chiefs. He shall deliver an oration exhorting them with great zeal to be brave and courageous and never to be guilty of cowardice. At the conclusion of his oration he shall march forward and commence the War Song and he shall sing:

Now I am greatly surprised
And, therefore I shall use it—
The power of my War Song.
I am of the Five Nations
And I shall make supplication
To the Almighty Creator.
He has furnished this army.
My warriors shall be mighty
In the strength of the Creator.
Between him and my song they are
For it was he who gave the song
This war song that I sing!

82. When the warriors of the Five Nations are on an expedition against an enemy, the War Chief shall sing the War Song as he approaches the country of the enemy and not cease until his scouts have reported that the army is near the enemies' lines when the War Chief shall approach with great caution and prepare for the attack.

83. When peace shall have been established by the termination of the war against a foreign nation, then the War Chief shall cause all the weapons of war to be taken from the nation. Then shall the Great Peace be established and that nation shall observe all the rules of the Great Peace for all time to come.

84. Whenever a foreign nation is conquered or has by their own will accepted the Great Peace their own system of internal government may continue, but they must cease all warfare against other nations.

85. Whenever a war against a foreign nation is pushed until that nation is about exterminated because of its refusal to accept the Great Peace and if that nation shall by its obstinacy become exterminated, all their rights, property and territory shall become the property of the Five Nations.

86. Whenever a foreign nation is conquered and the survivors are brought into the territory of the Five Nations' Confederacy and placed under the Great Peace the two shall be known as the Conqueror and the Conquered. A symbolic relationship shall be devised and be placed in some symbolic position. The conquered nation shall have no voice in the councils of the Confederacy in the body of the Lords.

87. When the War of the Five Nations on a foreign rebellious nation is ended, peace shall be restored to that nation by a withdrawal of all their weapons of war by the War Chief of the Five Nations. When all the terms of peace shall have been agreed upon a state of friendship shall be established.

88. When the proposition to establish the Great Peace is made to a foreign nation it shall be done in mutual council. The foreign nation is to be persuaded by reason and urged to come into the Great Peace. If

the Five Nations fail to obtain the consent of the nation at the first council a second council shall be held and upon a second failure a third council shall be held and this third council shall end the peaceful methods of persuasion. At the third council the War Chief of the Five nations shall address the Chief of the foreign nation and request him three times to accept the Great Peace. If refusal steadfastly follows the War Chief shall let the bunch of white lake shells drop from his outstretched hand to the ground and shall bound quickly forward and club the offending chief to death. War shall thereby be declared and the War Chief shall have his warriors at his back to meet any emergency. War must continue until the contest is won by the Five Nations.

89. When the Lords of the Five Nations propose to meet in conference with a foreign nation with proposals for an acceptance of the Great Peace, a large band of warriors shall conceal themselves in a secure place safe from the espionage of the foreign nation but as near at hand as possible. Two warriors shall accompany the Union Lord who carries the proposals and these warriors shall be especially cunning. Should the Lord be attacked, these warriors shall hasten back to the army of warriors with the news of the calamity which fell through the treachery of the foreign nation.

90. When the Five Nations' Council declares war any Lord of the Confederacy may enlist with the warriors by temporarily renouncing his sacred

Lordship title which he holds through the election of his women relatives. The title then reverts to them and they may bestow it upon another temporarily until the war is over when the Lord, if living, may resume his title and seat in the Council.

91. A certain wampum belt of black beads shall be the emblem of the authority of the Five War Chiefs to take up the weapons of war and with their men to resist invasion. This shall be called a war in defense of the territory.

92. If a nation, part of a nation, or more than one nation within the Five Nations should in any way endeavor to destroy the Great Peace by neglect or violating its laws and resolve to dissolve the Confederacy, such a nation or such nations shall be deemed guilty of treason and called enemies of the Confederacy and the Great Peace.

   It shall then be the duty of the Lords of the Confederacy who remain faithful to resolve to warn the offending people. They shall be warned once and if a second warning is necessary they shall be driven from the territory of the Confederacy by the War Chiefs and his men.

93. Whenever a specially important matter or a great emergency is presented before the Confederate Council and the nature of the matter affects the entire body of the Five Nations, threatening their utter ruin, then the Lords of the Confederacy must submit the matter to the decision of their people

and the decision of the people shall affect the decision of the Confederate Council. This decision shall be a confirmation of the voice of the people.

94. The men of every clan of the Five Nations shall have a Council Fire ever burning in readiness for a council of the clan. When it seems necessary for a council to be held to discuss the welfare of the clans, then the men may gather about the fire. This council shall have the same rights as the council of the women.

95. The women of every clan of the Five Nations shall have a Council Fire ever burning in readiness for a council of the clan. When in their opinion it seems necessary for the interest of the people they shall hold a council and their decisions and recommendations shall be introduced before the Council of the Lords by the War Chief for its consideration.

96. All the Clan council fires of a nation or of the Five Nations may unite into one general council fire, or delegates from all the council fires may be appointed to unite in a general council for discussing the interests of the people. The people shall have the right to make appointments and to delegate their power to others of their number. When their council shall have come to a conclusion on any matter, their decision shall be reported to the Council of the Nation or to the Confederate

Council (as the case may require) by the War Chief or the War Chiefs.

97. Before the real people united their nations, each nation had its council fires. Before the Great Peace their councils were held. The five Council Fires shall continue to burn as before and they are not quenched. The Lords of each nation in future shall settle their nation's affairs at this council fire governed always by the laws and rules of the council of the Confederacy and by the Great Peace.

98. If either a nephew or a niece see an irregularity in the performance of the functions of the Great Peace and its laws, in the Confederate Council or in the conferring of Lordship titles in an improper way, through their War Chief they may demand that such actions become subject to correction and that the matter conform to the ways prescribed by the laws of the Great Peace.

99. The rites and festivals of each nation shall remain undisturbed and shall continue as before because they were given by the people of old times as useful and necessary for the good of men.

100. It shall be the duty of the Lords of each brotherhood to confer at the approach of the time of the Midwinter Thanksgiving and to notify their people of the approaching festival. They shall hold a council over the matter and arrange its details and begin the Thanksgiving five days after the moon of Dis-ko-nah is new. The people shall assemble

at the appointed place and the nephews shall notify the people of the time and place. From the beginning to the end the Lords shall preside over the Thanksgiving and address the people from time to time.

101. It shall be the duty of the appointed managers of the Thanksgiving festivals to do all that is needed for carrying out the duties of the occasions.

    The recognized festivals of Thanksgiving shall be the Midwinter Thanksgiving, the Maple or Sugar-making Thanksgiving, the Raspberry Thanksgiving, the Strawberry Thanksgiving, the Cornplanting Thanksgiving, the Corn Hoeing Thanksgiving, the Little Festival of Green Corn, the Great Festival of Ripe Corn and the complete Thanksgiving for the Harvest.

    Each nation's festivals shall be held in their Long Houses.

102. When the Thanksgiving for the Green Corn comes the special managers, both the men and women, shall give it careful attention and do their duties properly.

103. When the Ripe Corn Thanksgiving is celebrated the Lords of the Nation must give it the same attention as they give to the Midwinter Thanksgiving.

104. Whenever any man proves himself by his good life and his knowledge of good things, naturally fitted as a teacher of good things, he shall be recognized

by the Lords as a teacher of peace and religion and the people shall hear him.

105. The song used in installing the new Lord of the Confederacy shall be sung by Adodarhoh and it shall be:

   " " Haii, haii Agwah wi-yoh
   " " A-kon-he-watha
   " " Ska-we-ye-se-go-wah
   " " Yon-gwa-wih
   " " Ya-kon-he-wa-tha
   Haii, haii It is good indeed
   " " (That) a broom, —
   " " A great wing,
   " " It is given me
   " " For a sweeping instrument."

106. Whenever a person properly entitled desires to learn the Pacification Song he is privileged to do so but he must prepare a feast at which his teachers may sit with him and sing. The feast is provided that no misfortune may befall them for singing the song on an occasion when no chief is installed.

107. A certain sign shall be known to all the people of the Five Nations which shall denote that the owner or occupant of a house is absent. A stick or pole in a slanting or leaning position shall indicate this and be the sign. Every person not entitled to enter the house by right of living within it upon seeing such a sign shall not approach the house either by day or

by night but shall keep as far away as his business will permit.

108. At the funeral of a Lord of the Confederacy, say:

"Now we become reconciled as you start away. You were once a Lord of the Five Nations' Confederacy and the United People trusted you. Now we release you for it is true that it is no longer possible for us to walk about together on the earth. Now, therefore, we lay it (the body) here. Here we lay it away. Now then we say to you, 'Persevere onward to the place where the Creator dwells in peace. Let not the things of the earth hinder you. Let nothing that transpired while yet you lived hinder you. In hunting you once took delight; in the game of Lacrosse you once took delight and in the feasts and pleasant occasions your mind was amused, but now do not allow thoughts of these things to give you trouble. Let not your relatives hinder you and also let not your friends and associates trouble your mind. Regard none of these things.'

"Now then, in turn, you here present who were related to this man and you who were his friends and associates, behold the path that is yours also! Soon we ourselves will be left in that place. For this reason hold yourselves in restraint as you go from place to place. In your actions and in your conversation do no idle thing. Speak not idle talk neither gossip. Be careful of this and speak not and do not give way to evil behavior. One year is the time that you must abstain from unseemly levity but if you can not do this for ceremony, ten days is the time to regard these things for respect."

109. At the funeral of a War Chief, say:

"Now we become reconciled as you start away. You were once a War Chief of the Five Nations' Confederacy and the United People trusted you as their guard from the enemy." (The remainder is the same as the address at the funeral of a Lord.)

110. At the funeral of a Warrior, say:

"Now we become reconciled as you start away. Once you were a devoted provider and protector of your family and you were ever ready to take part in battles for the Five Nations' Confederacy. The United People trusted you." (The remainder is the same as the address at the funeral of a Lord.)

111. At the funeral of a young man, say:

"Now we become reconciled as you start away. In the beginning of your career you are taken away and the flower of your life is withered away." (The remainder is the same as the address at the funeral of a Lord.)

112. At the funeral of a chief woman, say:

"Now we become reconciled as you start away. You were once a chief woman in the Five Nations' Confederacy. You once were a mother of the nations. Now we release you for it is true that it is no longer possible for us to walk about together on the earth. Now, therefore, we lay it (the body) here. Here we lay it away. Now then we say to you,

'Persevere onward to the place where the Creator dwells in peace. Let not the things of the earth hinder you. Let nothing that transpired while you lived hinder you. Looking after your family was a sacred duty and you were faithful. You were one of the many joint heirs of the Lordship titles. Feastings were yours and you had pleasant occasions . . .'" (The remainder is the same as the address at the funeral of a Lord.)

113. At the funeral of a woman of the people, say:
"Now we become reconciled as you start away. You were once a woman in the flower of life and the bloom is now withered away. You once held a sacred position as a mother of the nation. (Etc.) Looking after your family was a sacred duty and you were faithful. Feastings . . . (etc.)" (The remainder is the same as the address at the funeral of a Lord.)

114. At the funeral of an infant or young woman, say:
"Now we become reconciled as you start away. You were a tender bud and gladdened our hearts for only a few days. Now the bloom has withered away . . . (etc.) Let none of the things that transpired on earth hinder you. Let nothing that happened while you lived hinder you." (The remainder is the same as the address at the funeral of a Lord.)

115. When an infant dies within three days, mourning shall continue only five days. Then shall you gather the little boys and girls at the house of mourning and at the funeral feast a speaker shall address the

children and bid them be happy once more, though by a death, gloom has been cast over them. Then shall the black clouds roll away and the sky shall show blue once more. Then shall the children be again in sunshine.

116. When a dead person is brought to the burial place, the speaker on the opposite side of the Council Fire shall bid the bereaved family cheer their minds once again and rekindle their hearth fires in peace, to put their house in order and once again be in brightness for darkness has covered them. He shall say that the black clouds shall roll away and that the bright blue sky is visible once more. Therefore shall they be in peace in the sunshine again.

117. Three strings of shell one span in length shall be employed in addressing the assemblage at the burial of the dead. The speaker shall say:

"Hearken you who are here, this body is to be covered. Assemble in this place again ten days hence for it is the decree of the Creator that mourning shall cease when ten days have expired. Then shall a feast be made."

Then at the expiration of ten days the speaker shall say:

"Continue to listen you who are here. The ten days of mourning have expired and your minds must now be freed of sorrow as before the loss of a relative. The relatives have decided to make a little compensation to those who have assisted at the funeral. It is a mere expression of thanks. This is to the one who did the cooking while the body was lying in the house. Let her come forward and receive this gift and be dismissed from the task." In substance this shall be repeated for every one who assisted in any way until all have been remembered.

Glossary

checks and balances—In government, a system whereby the powers of each branch are "checked," or limited, by another branch so power is balanced among them all.

clan—A political and social group within Iroquois nations, formed of related families.

confederacy—A union of nations; also called a confederation.

constitution—A written or unwritten system of laws and principles of government.

council—A governing body formed of delegates from the local units of a confederacy.

council fire—A special fire around which Iroquois government leaders met to do business.

democracy—A system of government in which the people hold the ruling power, usually through elected representatives.

Gayaneshakgowa—The Great Law of Peace; the story of the founding of the Iroquois Confederacy.

Grand Council—The term for the main ruling body in the Iroquois Confederacy. Sometimes called the Great Council or Confederacy Council.

Haudenosaunee—The Iroquois term for themselves, meaning "People of the Long House."

long house—A type of house built by the Iroquois before contact with Europeans. It was longer than it was wide, with a high door at each end and smoke holes in the roof.

matriarchy—A family or tribe headed by a woman, through whom lines of descent are traced.

moiety—One of two primary subdivisions of a group. The Iroquois Grand Council had two moieties, the Older Brothers and the Younger Brothers.

ohwachira—The family unit formed of all the children of a particular elder female and all descendants of her female children. Two or more ohwachiras form a clan.

ratify—To confirm or make official.

reservation—(called a reserve in Canada) Land set aside by the United States or Canadian government for native tribes.

sachem—A tribal chief or ruler. An Iroquois sachem is a chief, or lord, on the Grand Council.

stockade—A defensive barrier made of stakes driven side by side into the ground.

Tadadaho—An Onondaga chief who was once evil but reformed and became a sachem on the Grand Council. Sometimes spelled Adodarhoh.

tripartite—Divided into three parts.

veto—To refuse to approve a bill or resolution so that it does not become law.

wampum—Small beads made of white or purple shells. The Iroquois used wampum strings or belts to record matters of national importance and as money.

Further Reading

Dunbar-Ortiz, Roxanne. *An Indigenous Peoples'
History of the United States*. Boston: Beacon Press,
2014.

Fenton, William N. *The Great Law and the
Longhouse: A Political History of the Iroquois
Confederacy*. Norman, Okla.: University of
Oklahoma Press, 2010.

Jennings, Francis. *The Ambiguous Iroquois Empire*.
New York: W.W. Norton & Company, 2013.

Johnson, Michael. *Iroquois: People of the Longhouse*.
Richmond Hill, Ontario: Firefly Books, 2013.

Potts, Steve. *Iroquois*. Mankato, Minn.: Creative
Education, 2015.

Web Sites

iroquoismuseum.org

The Iroquois Indian Museum is an educational institution dedicated to fostering understanding of Iroquois culture. It is informed by research on archaeology, history, and the common creative spirit of modern artists and craftspeople.

oneida-nation.net

This Web site includes history, news, and culture regarding the Oneida.

indian.senate.gov

The Senate Committee on Indian Affairs proposes legislation to alleviate the unique challenges of the American Indian, such as education, economic development, land management, trust responsibilities, health care, and claims against the United States.

senecamuseum.org

The Web site of the Seneca-Iroquois National Museum features virtual tours of its permanent and temporary exhibits.

Chapter Notes

Chapter One. The Formation of a Confederacy

1. Iroquois Constitution, *University of Oklahoma Law Center* (http://www.law.ou.edu/hist/iroquois.html), retrieved December 5, 2001, paragraphs 1, 2.
2. John C. Mohawk, "Iroquois Confederacy," *Encyclopedia of North American Indians,* ed. Frederick E. Hoxie (Boston: Houghton Mifflin, 1996), p. 299.
3. Hanni Woodbury, Reg Henry, and Harry Webster, eds. and trans., "Concerning the League: The Iroquois League Tradition as Dictated in Onondaga by John Arthur Gibson," *Algonquian and Iroquoian Linguistics Memoir* 9 (Winnipeg, Manitoba: Algonquian and Iroquoian Linguistics, 1992), p. 29.
4. J. N. B. Hewitt, "Legend of the Founding of the Iroquois League," *American Anthropologist*, Vol. 5, April 1892, p. 136.
5. Ibid., p. 133.

6. Woodbury, et al., p. 30.

7. Horatio Hale, "A Lawgiver of the Stone Age," *Proceedings of the American Association for the Advancement of Science,* Vol. 30, 1882, p. 332.

8. Hewitt, p. 140.

Chapter Two. The Establishment of the Great Law of Peace

1. Iroquois Constitution, *University of Oklahoma Law Center* (http://www.law.ou.edu/hist/iroquois.html), retrieved December 5, 2001, paragraphs 9, 12.

2. J. N. B. Hewitt, "Legend of the Founding of the Iroquois League," *American Anthropologist*, Vol. 5, April 1892, p. 132.

3. Iroquois Constitution, paragraph 35.

4. Ibid., paragraph 6.

5. Ibid.

6. Ibid., paragraph 7.

Chapter Three. The Power of the Iroquois Constitution

1. Iroquois Constitution, *University of Oklahoma Law Center* (http://www.law.ou.edu/hist/iroquois.html), retrieved December 5, 2001, paragraphs 93–96.

2. Ibid., paragraphs 42, 44.

3. Ibid., paragraph 17.

4. Ibid., paragraph 18.

5. Quoted in Bruce Johansen and Roberto Maestas, *Wasi'chu: The Continuing Indian Wars* (New York: Monthly Review Press, 1979), p. 35.

Chapter Four. The Legacy of the Iroquois Confederacy

1. Iroquois Constitution, *University of Oklahoma Law Center* (http://www.law.ou.edu/hist/iroquois.html), retrieved December 5, 2001, paragraphs 55, 57.

2. Ibid., paragraph 76.

3. Ibid., paragraph 80.

4. Quoted in Sally Roesch Wagner, "The Iroquois Influence on Women's Rights," *Indian Roots of American Democracy*, ed. José Barreiro (Ithaca, N.Y.: Akwe: kon Press, 1992), p. 123.

5. Quoted in Bruce Johansen and Roberto Maestas, *Wasi'chu: The Continuing Indian Wars* (New York: Monthly Review Press, 1979), p. 39.

6. Patricia Holt, "Steinem Edits a History of U.S. Women," *San Francisco Chronicle*, April 19, 1998 (http://www.sfgate.com/cgibin/article.cgi?file=/chronicle/archive/1998/04/19/RV25326.DTL), retrieved April 1, 2002, p. 2.

Index